C/C++ Software Development with Eclipse

Build v0.8.01-cae5c6a   *2014.01.07*

Purnank Harjivanbhai Ghumalia
&
Meera Purnank Ghumalia

Built with Ratatouille v0.5.03-cbc8dd1

(http://www.purnank.in/ratatouille/)

C/C++ Software Development with Eclipse by **Purnank Harjivanbhai Ghumalia & Meera Purnank Ghumalia**

- **ISBN-13** 978-1453662113
- **ISBN-10** 1453662111

The designations covered under a trademarks are attributed in the *section on Trademark Attribution* (Appendix H, on page 175).

Contents

Sisters

&

Brothers

Of the World [1]

---

[1] Resonating with *Sisters and Brothers of America* by Swami Vivekananda (http://en.wikipedia.org/wiki/-Swami_Vivekananda)

Preface

About this book

C/C++ Software Development with Eclipse is a an easy to understand yet thorough guide on using Eclipse [2] for C/C++ Software Development.

This book is not about a traditional introduction to Eclipse. This book gives a *practical* introduction to Eclipse. It introduces the features of Eclipse in the logical order in which any C/C++ programmer would need them; use them.

The book is appeals to a wide range of audience:

- It can help a student/freshman who has just started programming
- It can help a full time programmer to be more productive with Eclipse
- It can help a seasoned programmer maintaining a huge software stack

This book is available in various format and sizes. To know more about them and get them, see *Different formats of the book* (Appendix B, on page 163).

About The Authors

From her experience both as a teacher and working for the Software industry, Meera brings a unique blend of imparting knowledge and learn technical details practical to Software Developers. When not busy enjoying life with her sweet daughter Dehlia, she studies new trends and developments in Software Engineering to closely monitor Software Engineering landscape at the horizon. She microblogs to her twitter stream @LeanReligion (http://twitter.com/-LeanReligion) and blog.dehlia.in (http://blog.dehlia.in)

Purnank was first introduced to Eclipse based IDE in 2003 with IBM(R) Websphere(TM). The early fascination and a gradual influence of a plethora of Eclipse based plugins convinced him more that a swiss knife for software is finally available. With ever increasing functionality of C/C++ Development Tooling within Eclipse, he though it is the right time to introduce a

---

[2] Eclipse has many variants. This book can be used for *most* variants based on Eclipse / CDT

majority of C/C++ developers what they are missing and started working on this book with his wife, Meera.

Contact the Author

The *contact details* (Appendix J, on page 178) are given in a separate section. Your feedback & queries are always welcome.

Organization of the book

This book has four parts:

1. *Introduction* (Part I, on page 14) is for the users who do not know Eclipse. Who have used other IDEs. Want to get familiar with Eclipse. Its terminologies. This part gives a brief overview of Eclipse.

2. *C/C++ Software Development* (Part II, on page 48) is the main core of the book. Focused on C/C++ Development. For the users who know C/C++ and want to use Eclipse.

   This part is divided into sub-parts.

   Sub Part 1 *Reading Code* (Chapter 6, on page 48) (*developers always do this.*)

   Sub Part 2 *Building Code* (Chapter 7, on page 89) (*essential for any new* [3] *software.*)

   Sub Part 3 *Editing Code* (Chapter 8, on page 109) (*something that adds to the bottom line.*)

   Sub Part 4 *Tweaking Eclipse/CDT* (Chapter 9, on page 131) (*play, don't fight, with the tool.*)

3. *More from Eclipse* (Part III, on page 137) is about using Eclipse IDE more extensively. Using it beyond coding/programming. Using it for over-all software engineering. Looking at the **I** in **IDE**

4. *Advanced Eclipse* (Part IV, on page 142) covers technical details on Eclipse.

---

[3] Code/Software new to the developer. This can also be an age old software undergoing maintenance.

Typographical Conventions

Filenames, User Entry, Menu Selection, are presented using the following style:

`eclipse.ini`, `-Xmx`, *Window* → *Preferences*,

Commands are represented as:

eclipse, **make all**

Warnings, Cautions, that represent limitations and relatively important information are presented in the following style:

> **Warning:** Pay close **attention** to the warning.

Additional notes are represented using following style:

Note: This is a note.

References to glossary terms are presented using the following style:

JVM (Appendix A, on page 161)

External URLs are presented using the following style: (There's a small difference in printed and electronic media.)

Eclipse (http://eclipse.org)

References to sections and chapters are presented using the following style:

Introduction (Part I, on page 14)

Part I

Introduction

## CHAPTER 1

What is Eclipse?

It is not easy to explain in few words what Eclipse™ is. (*Definitely, the Eclipse we are talking about is not an astronomical phenomenon. It is also not about Vampires.*) This book is about the *Software* Eclipse that can be extended to do almost anything.

To give technical details of Eclipse, we can throw many jargons to the reader. OSGI, Platform, Workspace, SWT, Run-time, plug-ins, PDE, etc. The architecture of Eclipse. How things get together within Eclipse. How it internally works. Instead, we would take a practical approach. We would try to hide the internals of Eclipse. We would see a quick highlight of what Eclipse can do.

Technically, Eclipse is a *plugin based framework.* As it is plugin based, it can be extended to do a lot of diverse things. Eclipse is not just a Java/J2EE IDE. It is also an IDE for web Development [1], Python [2], perl, PHP, Ruby on Rails [1], etc.

Eclipse is also not only a programming IDE. It is also,

- A chat client

    The IBM® Lotus Notes® Sametime® (http://www.lotus.com/sametime). [3]

- A bit-torrent client

    Azurus (now called Vuze) [4]

- Many of the Eclipse RCP (Rich Client Platform) based products

---

[1] Aptana® Studio 2 (http://www.aptana.org/)

[2] PyDev (http://pydev.org/)

[3] IBM Developer Works article on Eclipse RCP (http://www.ibm.com/developerworks/websphere/techjournal/-0608_xu/0608_xu.html)

[4] Building VUZE in Eclipse (http://wiki.vuze.com/w/Using_Eclipse)

Even for C/C++ Development, it has/had many variants. Basic Eclipse CDT, CodeWarror, Windriver, ARM DS-5, etc.

Figure 1.1: Eclipse is IDE for many languages other than Java and C/C++.

To summarize everything, Eclipse platform overview page [#ecl-pltfrm-overview] clearly says:

Eclipse is for *Nothing in particular, but everything in general.*

## CHAPTER 2

What makes Eclipse Different?

For the pessimistic, its just another piece of software. But there are many things that get together to make a great ecosystem. An ecosystem not only with community developers but also a strong support of the industry.

- The Eclipse Foundation (Section 2.1, on the current page)
- Open Source — Eclipse Public License (EPL) (Section 2.2, on this page)
- Strong Community of Developers (Section 2.3, on the next page)
- Plugin Based (Section 2.4, on the facing page)
- Platform Independent (Section 2.5, on page 18)
- IT IS FAST (Section 2.6, on page 18)

2.1 The Eclipse Foundation

The first credit goes to the Eclipse Foundation. It is a not-for-profit organization. It is the umbrella body. It is the driving body behind the complete Ecosystem. The body that takes utmost care to keep Eclipse vendor-neutral.

You can read more about The Eclipse Foundation in detail at http://www.eclipse.org/org/

2.2 Open Source — Eclipse Public License (EPL)

Note: I am not legal expert. Please talk to your legal adviser for further clarifications.

EPL is not *Yet Another Open Source License*. On the middle ground, it is both industry-friendly and an OSI Approved Open Source license. [1] (And, EPL seems to lean toward industry.) For industry, it is like *best of both the worlds*. EPL is an OSI Approved License.

The EPL makes it easier for Industry to have proprietary systems based on Eclipse. (The terms of GPL conflict with the terms of EPL.)

Read more about EPL http://www.eclipse.org/org/documents/epl-v10.php and FAQs on EPL at http://www.eclipse.org/legal/eplfaq.php

Note: Again, I am not legal expert. Please talk to your legal adviser for further clarifications.

2.3 Strong Community of Developers

An open source software can never survive without a dedicated strong technical development community. There is a strong active community of developers and vendors that always look forward to a better Eclipse day-by-day.

Eclipse itself is divided into many parts. e.g. CDT is the part that focuses on adding features for C/C++, JDT is for JAVA. Different people, either volunteers or sponsored by industry work on these parts.

You can find more about the different projects at http://www.eclipse.org/downloads/-index_project.php

2.4 Plugin Based

What does plugin based mean? The concept is easy to see, but difficult to explain in words.

With plugins, you can extend the functionality of Eclipse. E.g. the CDT plugin adds functionality for C/C++ Development. Pydev plugin helps for Python development. Developers have the flexibility to use a wide range of configuration management tools right within Eclipse. The plugins make it a feature rich offering.

More about plugins is described in detail in *Plugins* (Chapter 15, on page 146).

To see the wide variety of plugins available for Eclipse, refer to the The Eclipse Marketplace. (http://marketplace.eclipse.org/)

---

[1] http://www.opensource.org/licenses/eclipse-1.0.php

2.5 Platform Independent

It works on Windows, Linux, Mac, etc. The look and feel is kept *native*. But the functionality remains the same.

2.6 IT IS FAST

We are not here for any flame wars.

Slow and *Fast* are relative terms. What are you comparing Eclipse with? Something that has *so many features*? Something that is platform independent. Something that would not only be your C/C++ Editor but also Java, Perl, PHP, JavaScript Editor? Some thing that can be extended to to *much more,* (Part III, on page 137) than just programming? The debate is endless.

If you already have made your mind that Eclipse is slow, there is nothing more to be done to convince you. But, it would be worth to see the Eclipse nightly builds page [2] . The performance of the plugins is monitored closely during these builds. This makes it easy for developer to notice that bug fixes do not add performance issues. It gives motivation to keep the builds fast.

---

[2] Eclipse builds (http://download.eclipse.org/eclipse/downloads/)

CHAPTER **3**

Installing Eclipse

3.1 Java

Java is a pre-requisite for Eclipse. If you don't have java installed on your system, download it from http://www.java.com

> **Warning:** On Linux, there maybe some issues with GCJ. (Eclipsepedia entry on GCJ. (http://wiki.eclipse.org/SDK_Known_Issues#Eclipse_using_GCJ))

3.2 Eclipse

Eclipse can be downloaded from http://eclipse.org/downloads.

Figure 3.1: The screenshot of www.eclipse.org/download

As shown in *The screenshot of www.eclipse.org/download* (Figure 3.1, on page 20), it is interesting to see how many different variants of Eclipse are available. Eclipse is extensible. Also, being based on Java, Eclipse can run a wide variety of platforms. Be it Linux / Macintosh or Windows. Since we are targeting C/C++ Development, please download the *C/C++* variant of Eclipse from http://eclipse.org/downloads for your system.

Note: If you already have Eclipse, and just want to *extend* it to have C/C++ development functionality, please refer *installing CDT.* (Section 16.2, on page 149)

3.3 Windows

> **Warning:** There maybe some issues with Windows extraction utility. (Eclipsepedia entry on Zip (http://wiki.eclipse.org/SDK_Known_Issues#Extracting_the_ZIP_file_fails)) Please use 7-Zip (http://www.7-zip.org) or other Zip utility.

Once you have downloaded the archive, unzip it to, say, `C:\eclipse`. Now you can start Eclipse by double clicking on `C:\eclipse\eclipse.exe`.

3.4 Linux - 32bit

```
cd /opt
tar -xvzf /path/to/eclipse-cpp-galileo-SR1-linux-gtk.tar.gz

# You can now run Eclipse IDE as /opt/eclipse/eclipse
```

3.5 Linux - 64bit

If you are using 64bit Linux *and 64bit JVM* download the 64bit version of Eclipse. If your JVM is 32bit, you can use the *32 bit version of Eclipse for Linux* (Section 3.4, on this page).

```
cd /opt
tar -xvzf /path/to/eclipse-cpp-galileo-SR1-linux-gtk-x86_64.tar.gz

# You can now run Eclipse IDE as /opt/eclipse/eclipse
```

3.6 Mac OS-X

Download the appropriate archive for Cocoa from http://eclipse.org/downloads and unzip to a folder of your choice. You can start Eclipse by clicking the Eclipse icon. For your convenience, you may also choose drag and drop the Eclipse icon to your launch dock.

3.7 Modifying default start-up settings

The default start-up settings for Eclipse are used from `eclipse.ini`. It is kept in the same directory as `eclipse.exe` (in Windows) or `eclipse` (in Linux).

A part of the default `eclipse.ini` looks *similar to* this:

```
1   -vmargs
2   -Dosgi.requiredJavaVersion=1.5
3   -Xms40m
4   Xmx256m
```

The default settings in `eclipse.ini` are (sometimes) very conservative.

If you are not aware of JVM parameters, here is what these settings mean:

`-Xms40m` = In the starting, JVM would need 40 MB memory

`-Xmx256` = If needed, JVM should be given 256 MB memory — Maximum.

Depending on the available free RAM on your system, the size of software stack you are developing, you can extend `eclipse.ini`. All new instances of Eclipse would respect these settings. This would help improve the performance of Eclipse.

This is how an updated `eclipse.ini` may look like.

```
1   -vmargs
2   -Dosgi.requiredJavaVersion=1.5
3   -Xms100m
4   -Xmx800m
```

This is what's changed:

`-Xms100m` = When Eclipse starts, JVM would need 100 MB memory.

`-Xmx700` = JVM should be given 700 MB memory — Maximum.

-Xms and -Xmx

-Xms

A low value of -Xms would mean, Eclipse starts with a less memory. *(The default value is sufficient for a small projects.)* But if you are using Eclipse for a relatively huge software stack, Eclipse would need more memory. Eclipse suddenly has to go back to the OS and request for more memory. This overhead would impact the overall performance of the system.

-Xmx

-Xmx is used to put a cap on the total memory that Eclipse would be allowed to use. Eclipse would not use this memory *always*. But if need arises, OS would give this memory to Eclipse.

Warning: If you request more than physical memory available on your system, virtual memory would be used. This would severely degrade the system performance.

You can also change other parameters for JVM. More at this entry on Eclipsepedia (http://wiki.eclipse.org/Eclipse.ini)

3.8 Upgrading Eclipse

Eclipse has a good and easy upgrade mechanism. You can update/upgrade Eclipse and the installed plugins. Please see more in separate chapter at *Upgrading Eclipse* (Chapter 14, on page 145)

3.9 Installing Tool-Chains

Eclipse does not ship with toolchains. On Linux, this is not an issue since compilers/linkers/debuggers are part of default configuration. On Windows, you will have to install some extra packages.

- Compiler/Linker
- Make utility
- Debugger

More at *Installing Tool-chains* (Appendix D, on page 166)

CHAPTER **4**

Starting Eclipse

You can start Eclipse from the Run menu as

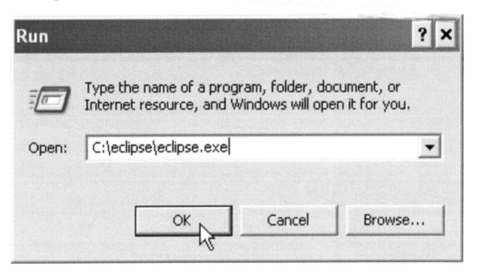

Figure 4.1: Starting Eclipse in windows

Note: Depending on installation of Eclipse, the path may vary.

First you will get the splash screen.

Then you would be asked to choose an *eclipse workspace* (Section 5.1, on page 30).

Figure 4.2: Eclipse splash screen

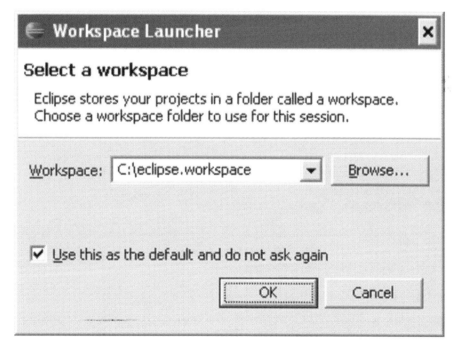

Figure 4.3: Selecting a workspace in Eclipse

Then you will get the Eclipse Welcome Screen. The welcome screen is only shown for the first time. After that you will always see *The default view of Eclipse* (Figure 4.5, on the facing page)

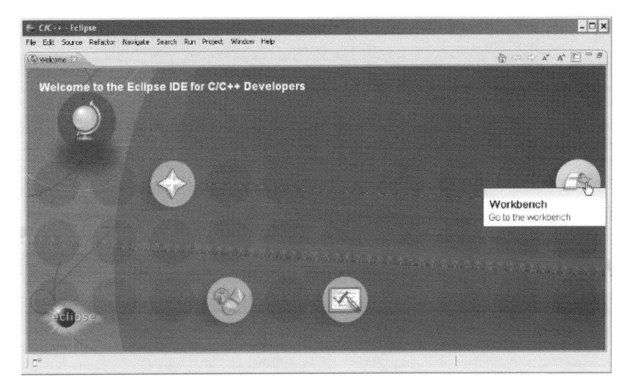

Figure 4.4: Eclipse welcome screen

As shown in the image, go to the workbench. You will see the normal Eclipse screen.

4.1 Different ways of starting Eclipse

These are some of the different ways you can start the Eclipse IDE.

You can start it:

- From the GUI. Double click on Eclipse executable
- Command line or the Run menu. Execute **eclipse** command. *(If the* **eclipse** *command is in path.)*

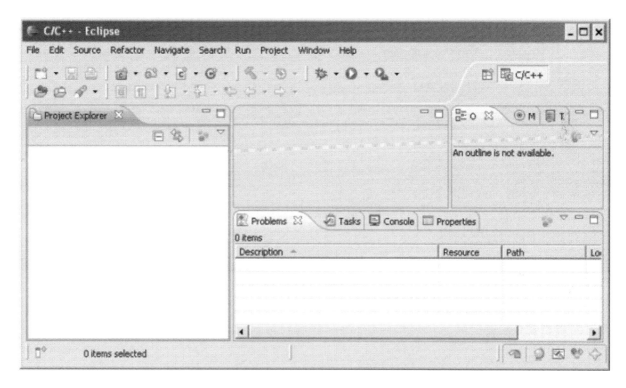

Figure 4.5: The default view of Eclipse

On Windows, you maybe able to use either of the command depending on where you installed Eclipse or what your path settings are.

```
C:\eclipse\eclipse.exe

eclipse.exe

eclipse
```

Similarly, for Linux

```
/opt/eclipse/eclipse

/home/user/opt/eclipse/eclipse

eclipse
```

For simplicity, we would use **eclipse** as the common command between Linux and Windows. And assume **eclipse** executable is in path.

- Pass optional command line arguments:

```
# eclipse -vmargs -Xmx<memory size>
eclipse -vmargs -Xmx700m
```

- For convinience, we can also create separate desktop shortcuts with *Eclipse specific startup settings* (Section 4.2, on the next page).

4.2 Changing the startup behaviour

Java Settings

Eclipse is based on Java. You can change settings that effect Java.

- The *Java Virtual Machine* (Appendix A, on page 161) used:

```
eclipse -vm c:\java6\jre\bin\javaw
```

- Amount of startup memory allocated:

```
eclipse -vmargs -Xms100m
```

- Amount of maximum memory allocated to Eclipse:

```
eclipse -vmargs -Xmx700m
```

- Other JVM parameters:

```
eclipse -vmargs -XX:MaxPermSize=400m -Xms100m -Xmx700m
```

Eclipse specific startup settings

- The *workspace* (Section 5.1, on the next page) used by Eclipse:

  ```
  eclipse -data x:/secure/eclipse.workspace
  ```

- Clean up the meta data:

  ```
  eclipse -data x:/secure/eclipse.workspace -clean
  ```

- Etc.

More about starting Eclipse can be found at this Eclipsepedia page (http://wiki.eclipse.org/-FAQ_How_do_I_run_Eclipse%3F)

## CHAPTER 5

Eclipse basics

This chapter would make you familiar with the terminologies of Eclipse. There is no rocket science in it. But the more you know, the merrier. You may not become an expert on Eclipse by reading this chapter, but this will help understand how things work in Eclipse.

5.1 Workspace

A workspace is like an *intermediate directory* for your Eclipse. Eclipse would use workspace as a cache for many of its operations. Preferences and settings also get stored into workspace.

The concept of a workspace is a little bit tricky. Why exactly is a workspace needed? Many tools need a location to store temporary but persistent data. These tools keep it hidden from the user. Eclipse makes user aware of this fact that there is actually something called a workspace.

For those engineers who can read UML, see the *Correlation of workspace, projects, resources, folders and files* (Figure 5.1, on the facing page).

A workspace can have many projects. Projects have folders and files. Workspace contains resources. Project, folders and files are *workspace resources* (Section 5.1, on the next page).

Note: Just to remain away from complexity, the relation between Eclipse and workspace has not been shown deliberately. For the beginning, it is assumed that developer would just use a single Eclipse workspace. The topic of multiple workspaces has been covered in detail in *another section.* (Chapter 13, on page 142)

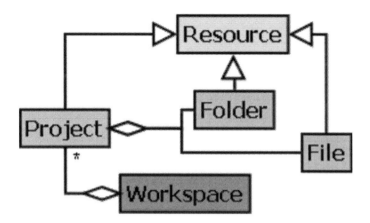

Figure 5.1: Correlation of workspace, projects, resources, folders and files

By default, new projects get created in workspace[1]. The default workspace is in user's home directory.

Selecting default workspace

When Eclipse first starts, Eclipse requests to select a workspace (See *Making workspace choice permanent* (Figure 5.2, on the next page)). Depending on the size of the projects, select an appropriate folder. Select *Use this as the default and do not ask again.* If needed, this selection can be reverted from *Create preferences to use a default workspace* (Section 13.4, on page 143)

Note: *No user serviceable parts inside.* Technically, there is nothing within Eclipse workspace for user to see/modify.

Resource

Conceptually, anything that is physically present in the file system can be an Eclipse resource. That includes a folder, file and the project itself.

There are two kinds of resources, ordinary resources & linked resources. The concept of linked files and folders is covered in *Creating a sample project* (Section 5.2, on page 33).

---

[1] User can also create projects outside Eclipse workspace.

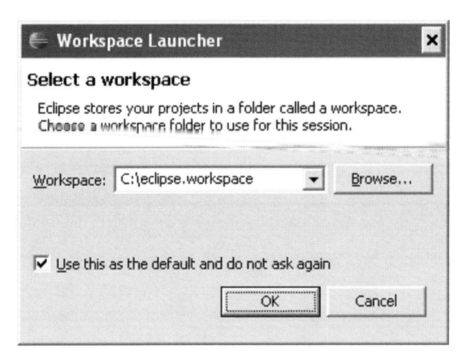

Figure 5.2: Making workspace choice permanent

5.2 Projects

Eclipse is not an editor. It's an IDE. Everything begins with a project.

This chapter would give an overview on using them in Eclipse.

Creating a sample project

Projects can be created via *File → New → Project*. Depending on the current *perspective* (Section 5.8, on page 45), the options in the file menu would change.

e.g. when you are in CDT Perspective, Eclipse would look like this:

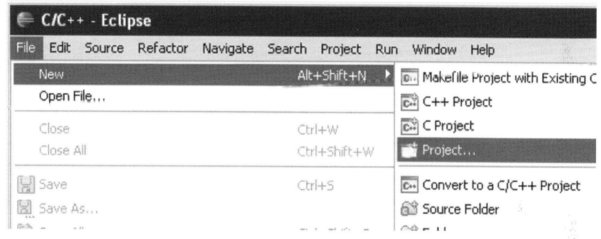

when you are in Resource Perspective, Eclipse would look like this:

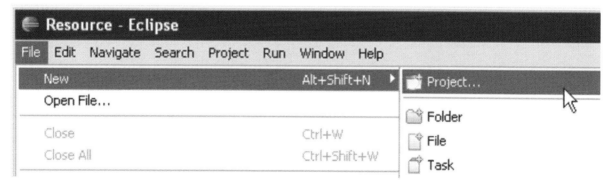

To keep things simple, we would create a general (Normal) project. We would create C/C++ Projects once we cover CDT in further detail.

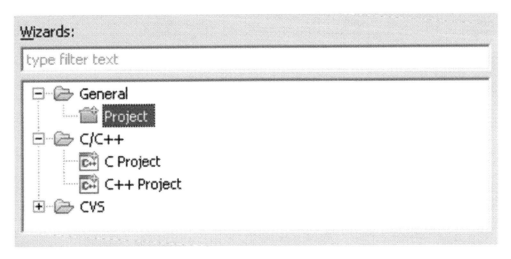

Name it as `DemoProject`

5.3 Create File

Let's create a new file `file.rtf`. There are many options to do that. *File* → *New* or `Right Click on the project`

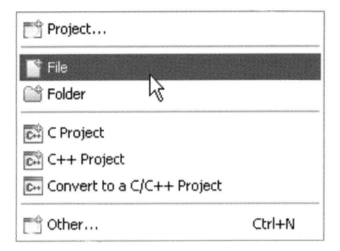

Name the file `file.rtf`

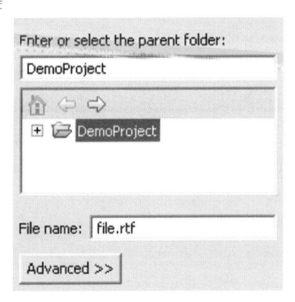

The file can be seen in the Eclipse *Project Explorer* (Section 5.7, on page 42).

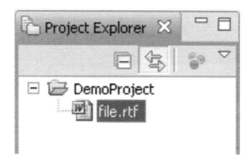

5.4 Create Folder

Similarly, we can also create a Folder. Let's create `source/documentation` folder It is note-worthy to see that we can easily create recursive folders.

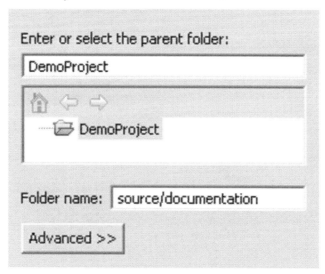

The Project Explorer view will show the new directory created.

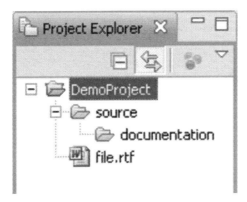

Using the Project Explorer, we can also move files and folders here and there.

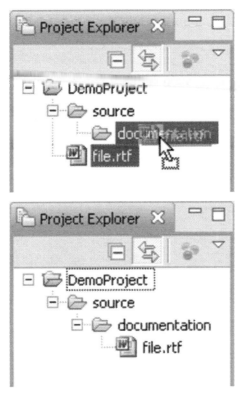

5.5 Linked Files and Folders

Eclipse also supports a feature of `linked files` and `linked folders`.

Linked files are similar to the concept of links in Linux and shortcuts in Windows. This is very handy feature for large software projects with very complex organization. The uses are limit-less. We can create link to a file/folder within the project, or outside the Project.

Let's create a link to the existing file.rtf

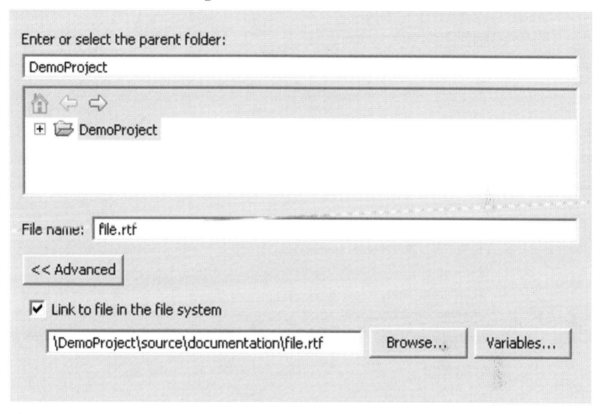

This is how it would look in *Project Explorer* (Section 5.7, on page 42)

The information about these linked files/folders is stored in `.project`

5.6 Opening Files

To opening the file... `double click.` or drag and drop to the editor.

Sometimes, all files *may not* open directly into the editor. They are opened by the *default system editor* instead. e.g. The `file.rtf`. When double clicked it, it may open with opens in the default editor. What if you want to open it within Eclipse?

Right click → Open with

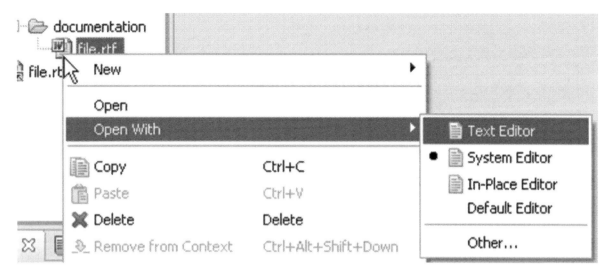

To edit the file with system default editor, select *System Editor*. Or choose *Other...* to edit file with some other editor.

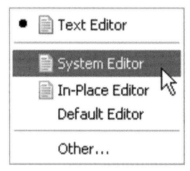

Eclipse also supports, `In place editor`. It means, the file is being edited by the `system editor` but within Eclipse IDE.

The leading `dot` in the context menu means the file was previously opened with `Text Editor`

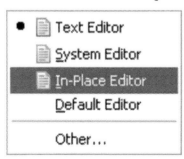

`file.rtf` being edited in in-place-editor

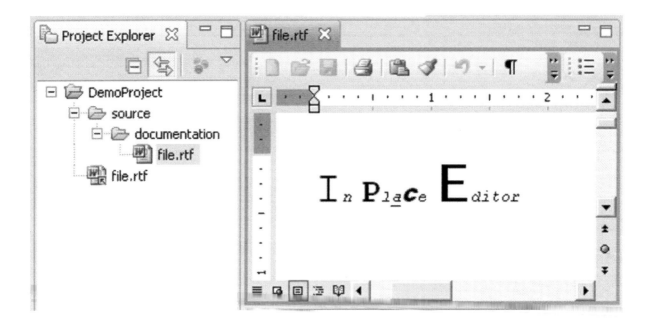

5.7 Views

A view is a *presentation* of data/information. Let's take an example:

Project Explorer

One of views shown in *previous section* (Section 5.3, on page 35) is the *Project Explorer* view. It gives a *tailored* presentation of the file system. Why *tailored?* It's *little* different from exactly what's present on the file system. You can also customize the view.

This is how a normal Project Explorer looks.

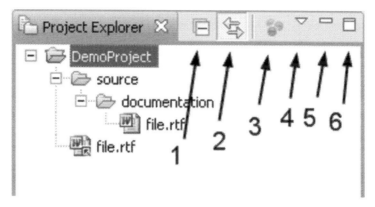

Here is an explanation on the meaning of the icons on top right corner of the view.

1. Minimize the display of all projects in this view.

2. Link the *editor* with this view. e.g. if `file.rtf` is opened in editor the project explorer would select that file automatically.

   This is useful if we want to find where the opened file is physically present within the project.

3. Enable MyLyn for this view. [2]

4. Access to further options

5. Minimize this view (And all views stacked behind)

6. Maximize this view (and all views stacked behind) in Eclipse window

Click on *Button 4*. A menu like this will pop up.

---

[2] Mylyn is a task-focused interface for Eclipse that reduces information overload and makes multitasking easy. More at http://www.eclipse.org/mylyn/

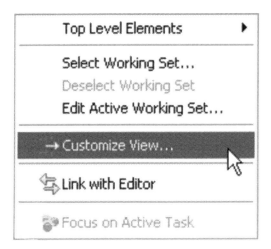

Uncheck the *.resources* (pointed by the arrow.)

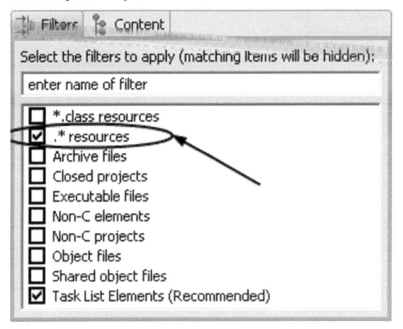

Now, you can see the hidden files with (a leading .) In this case, the .project

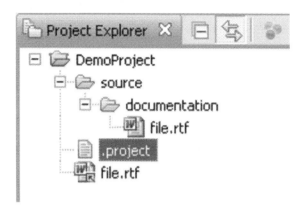

Open a view

Eclipse has many internal views. (The added plugins can contribute to more views). A view can be opened as wished. The available basic views can be opened from *Window → Show View*. More entries can be found from *Window → Show View → Other* or the keyboard shortcut Alt + Shift + Q, Q

5.8 Perspectives

A perspective is a set of *Views* (Section 5.7, on page 42). e.g. Eclipse has C/C++ perspective and Debug perspective

Why do we need perspectives? Take an example. While developing code, user would be interested in Tasks, Bookmarks, Compilation Warnings/Errors but, while debugging the code, these are totally irrelevant things. On the other hand, Breakpoints, Local Variables, Watch Expressions become much more important.

A perspective can be termed as the look of Eclipse. When user jumps around from C/C++ perspective and Debug perspective (or any other perspective), the look changes.

Perspectives can be controlled from *Window* in menubar.

- *Window → Open Perspective* — Select a perspective

- *Window → Show View* — Add a view to the current perspective

- *Window → Save Perspective As* — Create a custom perspective

- *Window → Reset Perspective* — Remove the customization

Once a view is opened, Eclipse remembers it and associates it with that perspective.

Part II

C/C++ Software Development

## CHAPTER 6

Reading Code

This is what developers do every time.

- They read the code.

- Read the lines of code others have written.

- Other developer's code for code maintenance.

- The API Signatures / Function prototypes

- The values of constants.

- They read the same code written *just few minutes back.*

Note: Hello World Vs. Zlib

Eclipse is *more than what meets the eye* (Chapter 1, on page 14). To cover all the features of Eclipse, A *Hello World* project would not be enough. We have chosen *Zlib*. The examples / screen shots shown in this book are from *Zlib*

If you want to take *Do-It-Yourself* approach along with this book, refer to *Setting up Zlib Source* (Appendix E, on page 169) and then come back to this chapter.

This is how an opened file, `example.c` would look in Eclipse.

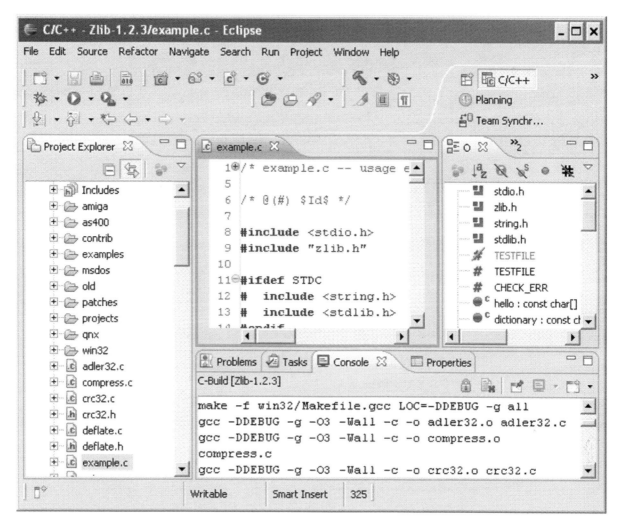

These are the topics discussed in further detail:

6.1 Line Numbers

Where do we see the line numbers in Eclipse? *Not the most difficult thing to answer.*

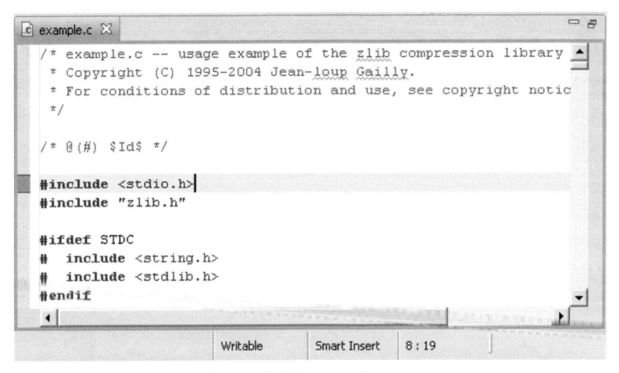

In the image, we can see 8:19. Line — 8, Column — 19.

If you want to see in the side bar, easy! Just *Right Click* on the left pane of the editor and select *Show Line Numbers*

A rather complicated way to toggle line numbers is via *Window* → *Preferences* → *General* → *Editors* → *Text Editors*

6.2 Code Folding

With this feature, we can reduce the code to outlines. To enable folding in current source file, *Right Click → Folding → Enable Folding*.

Eclipse can also *fold* code, as soon as the source file is opened. To enable it, open *Window → Preferences → C/C++ → Editor → Folding*. Be careful with this feature, for huge files it maybe resource intensive.

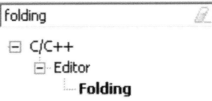

folding

☐ C/C++
  ☐ Editor
    Folding

☑ Enable folding when opening a new editor

Select folding to use: Default C Folding ▼

☑ Enable folding of preprocessor branches (#if/#endif)
☑ Enable folding of control flow statements (if/else, do/while, for, switch)

Initially fold these region types:
☑ Macros
☐ Functions
☐ Methods
☑ Structures
☐ Comments
☑ Header Comments
☑ Inactive Preprocessor Branches

Most of the options in the preferences are self-explanatory.

See that there is a separate provision to hide *license / copyright* related header comment at the beginning of the source file by default. This feature will automatically hide just the license/copyright headers at the beginning of the source file, but show other relevant comments.

Note: The folding of preprocessor branches may not work as expected some times.

Indexing might have to be setup correctly. See *Indexing* (Section 9.2, on page 132)

This is how folded inactive preprocessor branch would look like.

```
.c example.c ⊠
85⊖ void test_gzio(fname, uncompr, uncomprLen)
86      const char *fname; /* compressed file name */
87      Byte *uncompr;
88      uLong uncomprLen;
89  {
90⊕ #ifdef NO_GZCOMPRESS□
92⊖ #else
93      int err;
94      int len = (int)strlen(hello)+1;
95      gzFile file;
96      z_off_t pos;
```

This how fully collapsed code would look.

```
.c example.c ⊠
207⊕ void test_inflate(compr, comprLen, uncompr, uncomprLen)□
244
246⊕ * Test deflate() with large buffers and dynamic change of compression level□
248⊕ void test_large_deflate(compr, comprLen, uncompr, uncomprLen)□
299
301⊕ * Test inflate() with large buffers□
303⊕ void test_large_inflate(compr, comprLen, uncompr, uncomprLen)□
340
342⊕ * Test deflate() with full flush□
344⊕ void test_flush(compr, comprLen)□
378
380⊕ * Test inflateSync()□
382⊕ void test_sync(compr, comprLen, uncompr, uncomprLen)□
422
```

Keyboard Shortcuts

These are the default keyboard shortcuts for Code folding

- Enable Folding — Ctrl + Numpad Divide
- Expand All — Ctrl + Numpad Multiply
- Collapse All — Ctrl + Shift + Numpad Divide
- Reset Structure — Ctrl + Shift + Numpad Multiply

6.3 Outline View

The outline view gives a quick outline of the complete source file.

- What source files is it including?
- What are the variables in this file?
- What are the functions?
- Classes?
- Etc.

Here is the *Outline view of example.c* (Figure 6.1, on the facing page)

This view can be configured. The view has following buttons.

This is the explanation of each of them (from left to right).

1. Show the view sorted, not as in source file
2. Do not show fields (Member variables)
3. Do not show static members
4. Only show public members
5. Hide compiler/pre processor inactive switches

Similar to the *Project Explorer* (Section 5.7, on page 42), this view also has advanced preferences.

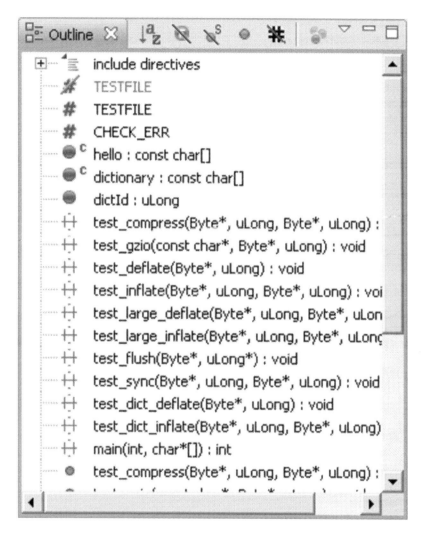

Figure 6.1: Outline view of example.c

If the outline view is linked to Eclipse Editor view, we can see the mapping between the two views. In the image below, selection of CHECK_ERR is synchronized between editor and outline. The left pane of the editor also gives a hint about the lines covered by CHECK_ERR.

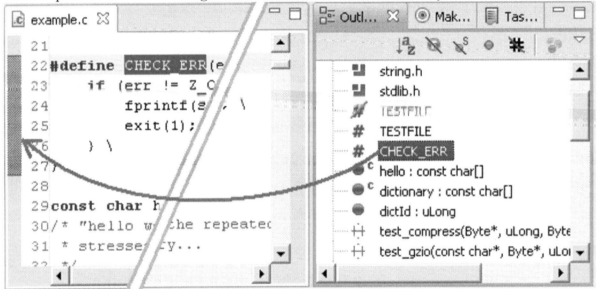

6.4 Quick Outline

What is quick outline?

Before we answer that question, another question.

- What is real estate?
- What is *screen* real estate?

There is a limited space on your screen. However big the screen maybe, it's still limited. Quick outline helps developer to get the outline of the source file *quickly*, and jump to needed point as fast as possible. A Real developer friendly feature. Developer does not need to do the boring scrolling down.

The keyboard shortcut to open it is `Control O`. (This keyboard short-cut will only work when you are *editing* a *C/C++* file.)

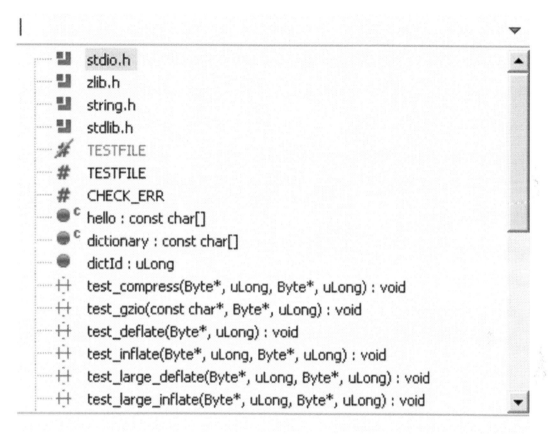

Figure 6.2: A quick outline view

6.5 Mark Occurrences

When a variable/function/identifier is *selected*, it helps to know where else it is being used.

In this image, variable `file` is selected in line `98`. The other locations where the same variable is used, also gets highlighted.

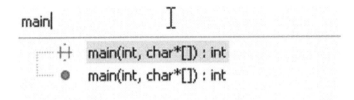

Figure 6.3: Jumping to a function.

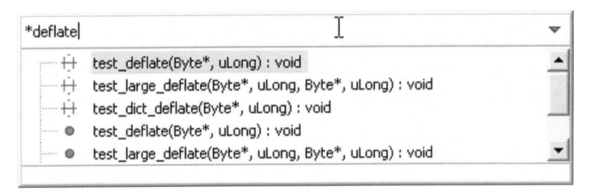

Figure 6.4: Using wild cards

```c
 95      gzFile file;
 96      z_off_t pos;
 97
 98      file = gzopen(fname, "wb");
 99      if (file == NULL) {
100          fprintf(stderr, "gzopen error\n");
101          exit(1);
102      }
103      gzputc(file, 'h');
104      if (gzputs(file, "ello") != 4) {
105          fprintf(stderr, "gzputs err: %s\n", gzerror(file, &err));
106          exit(1);
107      }
108      if (gzprintf(file, ", %s!", "hello") != 8) {
109          fprintf(stderr, "gzprintf err: %s\n", gzerror(file, &err));
110          exit(1);
111      }
112      gzseek(file, 1L, SEEK_CUR); /* add one zero byte */
113      gzclose(file);
```

When the references are spread across the file, a quick overview can also be found. As in this image, the occurrences are shown in the *right sidebar*. (See all the light blue markers on the right side of editor view.)

```
116   if (file == NULL) {
117        fprintf(stderr, "gzopen
118        exit(1);
119   }
120   strcpy((char*)uncompr, "garb
121
122   if (gzread(file, uncompr, (u
123        fprintf(stderr, "gzread
124        exit(1);
125   }
126   if (strcmp((char*)uncompr, h
127        fprintf(stderr, "bad gzr
```

Some times this feature is annoying. Its easy to disable/toggle it quickly.

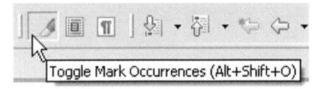

6.6 Quick Preview

Eclipse can show how a function is implemented. Just keep cursor on the function, Eclipse would show the implementation of that function.

```
 95      gzFile file;
 96      z_off_t pos;
 97
 98      file = gzopen(fname, "wb");
 99      if (fil /* ================================================
100          fpr        Opens a gzip (.gz) file for reading or writing.
101          exi  */
102      }        gzFile ZEXPORT gzopen (path, mode)
103      gzputc(        const char *path;
104      if (gzp        const char *mode;
105          fpr  {
106          exi
107      }            return gz_open (path, mode, -1);
108      if (gzp  }
109          fprintf(stderr, "gzprintf err: %s\n", gzerror(file, &er
                                                        Press 'F2' for focus
```

If we press F2 or click on the preview window, we get access to the complete source code of the function, without going away from the original file.

6.7 Macro Expansion

Within the code of Zlib, infback9.c has few macros. Let's see an example of NEEDBITS.

```
#define NEEDBITS(n)                          \
    do {                                     \
        while (bits < (unsigned)(n))         \
            PULLBYTE();                      \
    } while (0)
```

But. the macro NEEDBITS depends on PULLBYTE

```
#define PULLBYTE()                           \
    do {                                     \
        PULL();                              \
        have--;                              \
        hold += (unsigned long)(*next++) << bits; \
        bits += 8;                           \
    } while (0)
```

The dependencies continue.

```
#define PULL()                               \
    do {                                     \
        if (have == 0) {                     \
```

```
        have = in(in_desc, &next);        \
        if (have == 0) {                   \
            next = Z_NULL;                 \
            ret = Z_BUF_ERROR;             \
            goto inf_leave;                \
        }                                  \
    }                                      \
} while (0)

#define Z_NULL   0

#define Z_BUF_ERROR    (-5)
```

Now. What does NEEDBITS(3) expand to?

Just hover cursor on the Macro. See the full expansion of the Macro.

```
 203      }
 284      NEEDBITS(3);
 285   ┌─────────────────────────────────────────────────┐
 286   │Macro Expansion                                   │
 287○  │do { \                                            │
 288○  │        while (bits < (unsigned)(3)) \            │
 289   │            do { \                                │
 290   │        do { \                                    │
 291   │        if (have == 0) { \                        │
 292   │            have = in(in_desc, &next); \          │
 293○  │            if (have == 0) { \                    │
 294   │                next = 0; \                       │
 295   │                ret = (-5); \                     │
 296   │                goto inf_leave; \                 │
 297   │                     Press "F2" for macro expansion steps│
       └─────────────────────────────────────────────────┘
```

If this is an information overflow, we can also see the expansion Step-by-Step. Press F2.

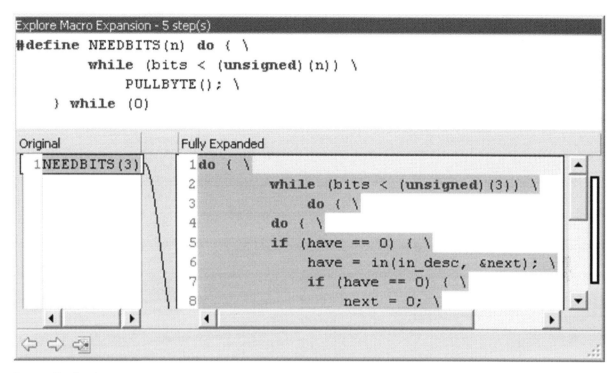

Press *Right Arrow* or Alt + Right to see step by step expansion.

Step 1/5:

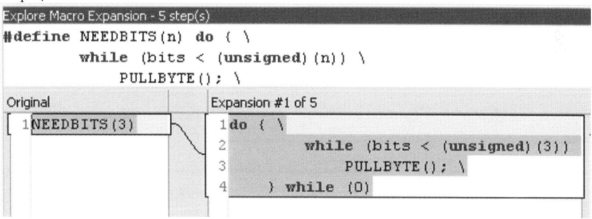

Step 2/5:

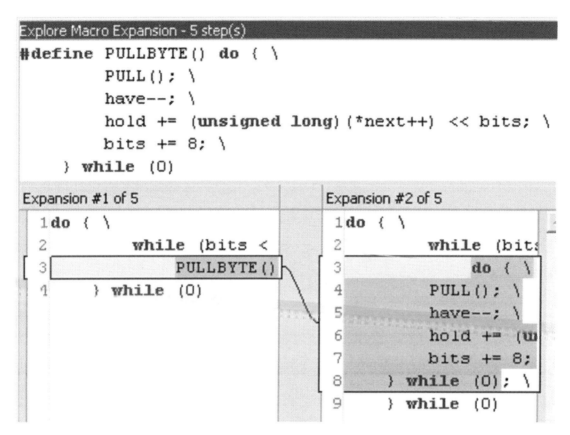

Step 3/5:

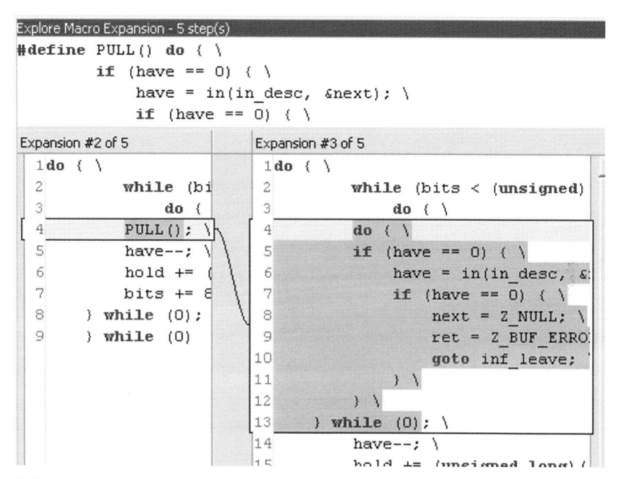

And so on...

6.8 Jumping within the file

If you want to jump around the source file, here are some of the quickly used keyboard shortcuts.

Action	Key
Next Member	Ctrl + Shift + Up
Previous Member	Ctrl + Shift + Down
Jump to Matching Bracket (Parenthesis)	Ctrl + Shift + P
Incremental find next	Ctrl + J
Incremental find previous	Ctrl + Shift + J
Next *Annotation* (Section 6.8, on the current page)	Ctrl + .
Previous *Annotation* (Section 6.8, on this page)	Ctrl + ,
Last edited place	Ctrl + Q
Previous cursor position.	Alt + Left
Next cursor position.	Alt + Right
Goto Line	Ctrl + L
Quick Outline (Section 6.4, on page 56)	Ctrl + O

Annotations

Annotations are *markers*. They are generated from the multiple sources like:

- Bookmarks

- Breakpoints

- C/C++ Indexing errors

- Search results

- Compiler errors/warnings

- FIXME/TODO Markers

- Etc.

When you press Ctrl + . (▾) / Ctrl + , (▾), you can go to the *next / previous* Annotation. You can enable/disable/skip certain annotations at your convenience.

From the drop down menu, you can *Select/Remove which annotation are selected for Jumps* (Figure 6.5, on the facing page). (The drop down menu is available when you press the small *down* button on the right of the ▾ or ▾ button.)

For improved visual feedback, it is also possible to configure how the annotations look. *General → Editors → Text Editors → Annotations* would take to *Annotation Preferences* (Figure 6.6, on the next page). Their meaning is shown in the next table.

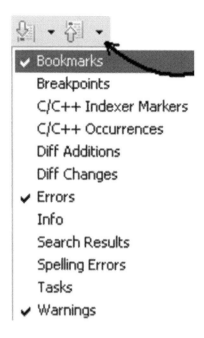

Figure 6.5: Select/Remove which annotation are selected for Jumps

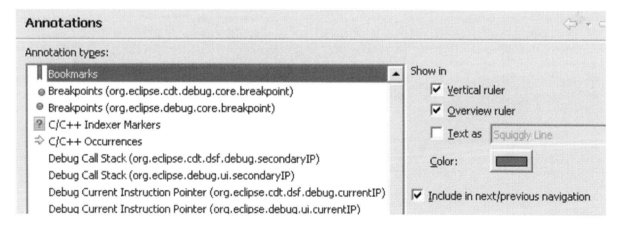

Figure 6.6: Annotation Preferences

Table 6.1: Preferences for Annotations

Vertical Ruler	Show the annotation marker on the left of editor.
Overview Ruler	Show the annotation overview on the right of editor.
Text As	Formatting of the text within editor.
Color	The color used for formatting within editor. And on the right overview ruler.
Include in...	Go to the marker when ⬇ ▾ ⬆ ▾ Ctrl + . Ctrl +, are pressed

6.9 Jumping to declaration/definition

C Language is strong typed language. Elements have a *declaration* and *definition*. Just press:

- F3
- Ctrl + Click
- *Navigate → Open Declaration*

Eclipse will take to the declaration/definition of the element.

```
65
66    err = compress(compr, &comprLen, (const Bytef*)hello, len);
67    CHECK_ERR(err, "compress");
68
69    strcpy((char*)uncompr, "garbage");
70
```

Just as we can *quickly open a file* (Section 6.10, on the facing page), we can also jump to any definition quickly. Ctrl + Shift + T / *Navigate → Open Element*

Choose an element (? = any character, * = any string):

zlib_*_mode

Visible element types:

☑ Ⓝ Namespace   ☑ Ⓒ Class   ☑ Ⓢ Struct   ☑ Ⓣ Typedef
☑ Ⓔ Enumeration   ☑ Ⓤ Union   ☑ ● Function   ☑ ● Variable
☑ # Macros

Matching elements:

\# ZLIB_FILEFUNC_MODE_CREATE
\# ZLIB_FILEFUNC_MODE_EXISTING
\# ZLIB_FILEFUNC_MODE_READ
\# ZLIB_FILEFUNC_MODE_READWRITEFILTER
\# ZLIB_FILEFUNC_MODE_WRITE

Qualified name and location:

\# (global) ZLIB_FILEFUNC_MODE_CREATE - /Zlib-1.2.3/contrib/minizip/ioapi.h

As shown in the image, there are options to filter the type of element.

Note: This feature heavily depends on *Indexing* (Section 9.2, on page 132)

6.10 Jumping across files

We work with an IDE, probably because the project is too huge to handle in small editors. Eclipse can help us quickly open files. This chapter gives an overview on easily navigating from one source file to another.

Opening existing file within project

Ctrl + Shift + r (Open Resource) is the handy keyboard shortcut. (*Navigate → Open Resource*)

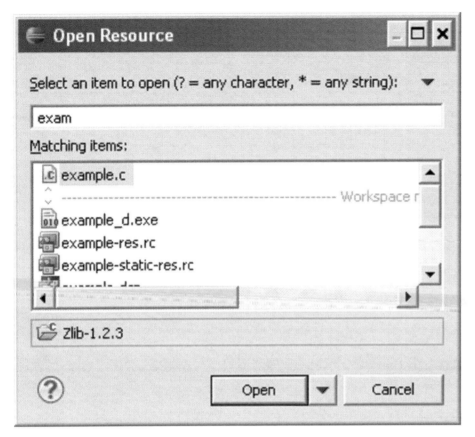

Just like *Quick Outline* (Section 6.4, on page 56) this view also supports wild cards.

Go to already open file

We mostly open more than one files. Sometimes we need to jump around to another file. An already open file. If we open many files, moving around becomes little difficult. This is how we move around files in Eclipse.

`Ctrl + E` — Jump to any Editor.

> **Warning:** `Ctrl + TAB` has a different use in Eclipse.

`Ctrl + PageUp` / `Ctrl + PageDown` can be used to go to next or previous editor.

Go to last edited File

Eclipse can quickly jump to last edited section. Just press `Ctrl + Q`. Eclipse would take us there.

6.11 Searching / Finding

A minority of *fresh* developers never look beyond simple `Ctrl + F`. Another minority of very experienced developers don't need to search. They have the complete code in their mind. They *may* know where each variable is used/declared in the project. This chapter is for a *majority* of the developers in between these two *minorities*.

This chapter would help you become a power user of search and thus more productive.

Simple Search

Basic search within the single source file.

`Ctrl + F` would bring up *Find/Replace Dialogue.* (Figure 6.7, on the next page).

The options are self explanatory. The same dialogue can be used to replace text.

If you know regular expressions, take full advantage of it. If you don't know, learn it.

Regular Expressions

This may not be the best example to show the full power of Regular Expressions, but here is a small example.

e.g. There is a *poor* code segment:

```
#define   uint8_t  unsigned char
#define    int8_t    signed char
#define uint16_t  unsigned short
#define   int16_t    signed short
#define uint32_t  unsigned int
#define   int32_t    signed int
```

During code-review, a fairly experienced C Developer would suggest to use `typedefs` instead of `#define`

Q How to do it quickly?

A Use *Regular Expressions* Use these values in *Find/Replace Dialogue.* (Figure 6.7, on the following page). We will get the desired output.

Find `#define\s+(\w+)\s+([\w ]+)$`

Replace With `typedef \2 \1;`

Figure 6.7: Find/Replace Dialogue.

If you can't remember the *syllables* of regular expressions, Eclipse would give *Assistance for regular expressions* (Figure 6.8, on the current page). Just press Ctrl + Space.

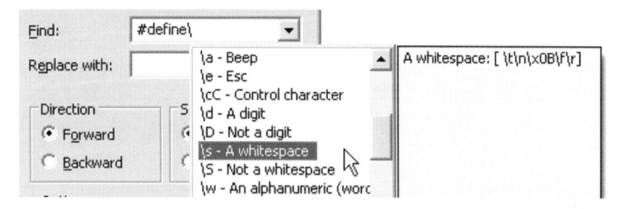

Figure 6.8: Assistance for regular expressions

Advanced Search

Beyond the *basic search* (Section 6.11, on page 71), Eclipse has supports an Extensive search feature. Press Ctrl + H or *Search → Search* to open the dialog.

Search within specific folder

To search within specific folder, change the Scope to *Selected Resources* in the *Search Dialog to search within Workspace* (Figure 6.9, on the next page)

C/C++ Sensitive Search

Just like *Advanced Search* (Section 6.11, on this page), Eclipse/CDT can also search C/C++ specific.

The options are self-explanatory. *Any Element* and *All Occurrences* would search all the types of Elements.

There is more than what meets the eye. Just like the scope resolution operator of C++, :: is the magic separator.

So, searching for *::in would find us all the class/structures that have in as the member field.

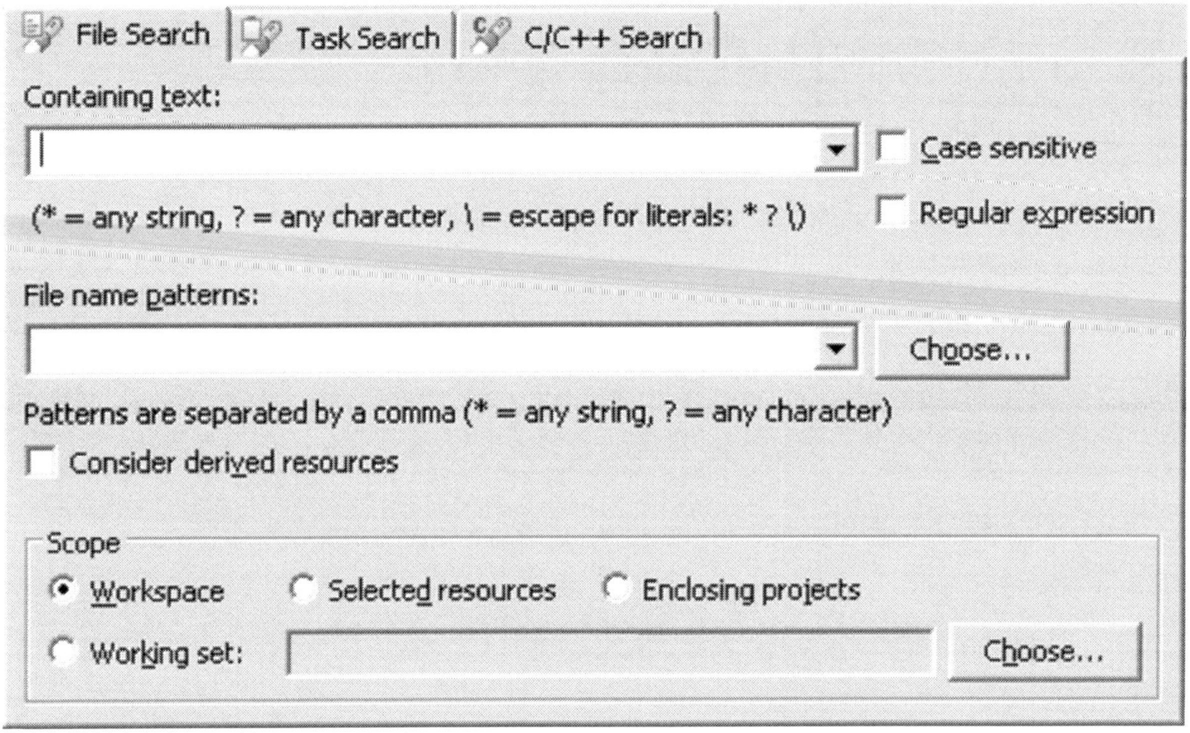

Figure 6.9: Search Dialog to search within Workspace

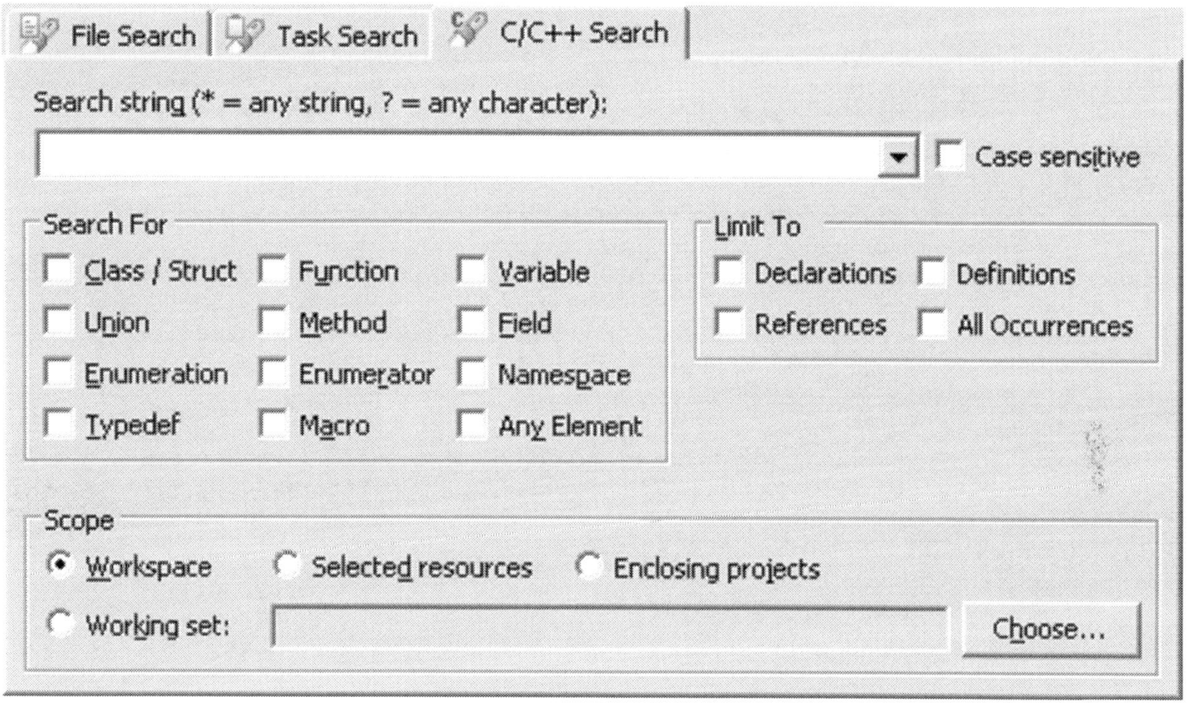

Figure 6.10: C/C++ Search

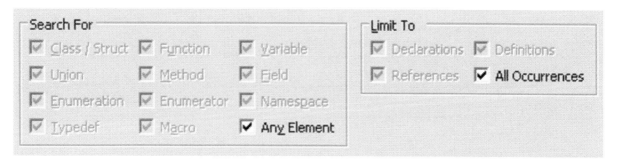

Figure 6.11: Disabled options when selected to search everything

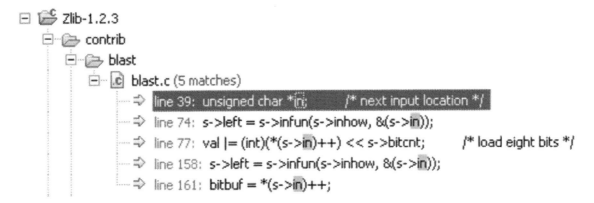

Figure 6.12: Searching for all usage of field in

We can also extend the view. From *Menu Options* 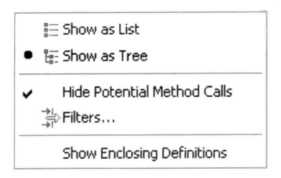, we to get *Advanced search options* (Figure 6.13, on the current page).

Figure 6.13: Advanced search options

If we enable *Show Enclosing Definitions*, we can *See the Search results with function/structure names* (Figure 6.14, on the facing page)

Similarly, with *Show as List*, we can *See the Search results in table format* (Figure 6.15, on the next page).

Quickly search references

`Ctrl + G` is a quick short-cut. Just select an element, and press `Ctrl + G`. Eclipse will quickly show us the contextual references of the given element.

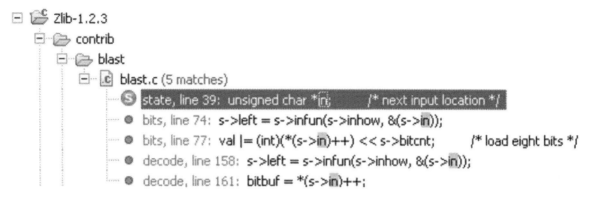

Figure 6.14: See the Search results with function/structure names

Location	Enclosing Definition		Match
⇨ /Zlib-1.2.3/contrib/blast/blast.c, line 39	Ⓢ	state	unsigned char *in; /* next input location */
⇨ /Zlib-1.2.3/contrib/blast/blast.c, line 74	●	bits	s->left = s->infun(s->inhow, &(s->in));
⇨ /Zlib-1.2.3/contrib/blast/blast.c, line 77	●	bits	val |= (int)(*(s->in)++) << s->bitcnt; /* load ei
⇨ /Zlib-1.2.3/contrib/blast/blast.c, line 158	●	decode	s->left = s->infun(s->inhow, &(s->in));
⇨ /Zlib-1.2.3/contrib/blast/blast.c, line 161	●	decode	bitbuf = *(s->in)++;
⇨ /Zlib-1.2.3/contrib/masmx64/inffas8664.c, line 86	Ⓢ	inffast_ar	/* 16 8 */ unsigned char FAR *in; /* esi rsi local sl

Figure 6.15: See the Search results in table format

To quickly go to the next/previous element, you may have to enable the *Annotations* (Section 6.8, on page 66)

Search View Options

The search results view has these advanced options:

The table below shows the explanation of the options.

Table 6.2: Advanced search options

Image	Action
⇩	Go to next search item (Ctrl + .)
⇧	Go to previous search item (Ctrl + ,)
✖	Remove the selected search item(s) from the search view
✖	Clear search results
🔍	Search/Find again
■	Stop searching
🔍 ▾	See previous search history
🗗	Pin the search view

Multiple Searches

Sometime we would like to search multiple items at the same time. e.g. What if we would like to search for zalloc and zfree at the same time?

Eclipse search has the feature called pinned search. In *Multiple search* (Figure 6.16, on the next page), *::zalloc search has been pinned, while *::zfree was searched later. Press the

🗗 (pin) button, and the search results would be *pinned*. The next search would be in a new view/window.

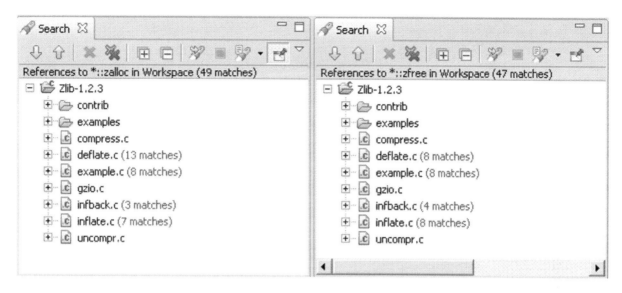

Figure 6.16: Multiple search

6.12 Call Hierarchy

Some times it is important to know who is calling this function (method). If the function is too huge, its also good to know what other functions are called by this function.

How to see it? *Right Click* on the function and select *Open Call Hierarchy*. The keyboard shortcut is Ctrl + Alt + H (*H* for *Hierarchy*).

This image tells what test_gzip is doing.

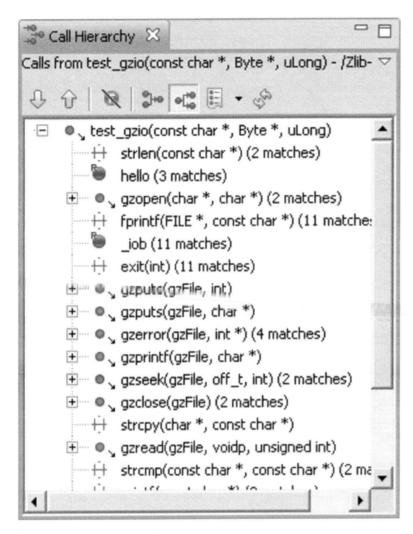

Here is an interpretation.

1. Calculating length of something. (`strlen`). But its done twice in this function. Use `Up` / `Down` arrows from the view Or `Ctrl + ,` / `Ctrl + .` to go to the source lines where it is used.

2. The variable `hello` is being read/modified. (Done at total 3 places)

3. Invokes `gzopen`. Done twice in this function. `gzopen` is doing something else internally too.

4. Etc.

You can toggle between who is calling this function / what functions are called by this function.

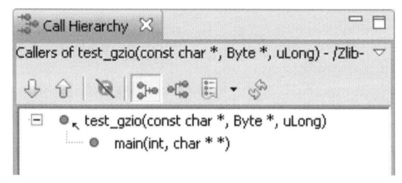

You can also toggle reads to field (variables), look at the recent history of call hierarchies looked, focus on another function.

6.13 Include browser

Which header files is this source file including? Who is including this header file? Directly? Indirectly?

Here is an view of *header files included by example.c* (Figure 6.17, on this page). As seen in figure, Windows.h is excluded from inclusion. A similar view for *zlib.h* (Figure 6.18, on the next page). The *opposite information* (Figure 6.19, on the following page) is also available.

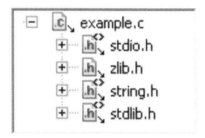

Figure 6.17: Header files included by `example.c`

This view is very similar to *Call Hierarchy* (Section 6.12, on page 79) and *Type Hierarchy* (Section 6.14, on page 83)

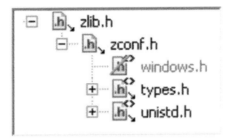

Figure 6.18: Header files included by zlib.h

Figure 6.19: Files that depend on zlib.h

6.14 Type Hierarchy

Inheritance is a basic concept of Object Oriented Programming. Unfortunately, the implementation is not *basic*. As the number of classes increases, it often becomes difficult to manage them. Which class is derived from which class. Which member functions does this class have? Its own? Inherited? Public? Private? Static?

Here is the *Type Hierarchy of a class* (Figure 6.20, on the current page) and *Type Hierarchy — with inherited members* (Figure 6.21, on the following page). We can also *Change the Layout of Type Hierarchy View* (Figure 6.22, on the next page).

To see the type hierarchy of the class, select the identifier and press F4. You can also use *Right Click → Open Type Hierarchy* , *Navigate → Open Type Hierarchy*

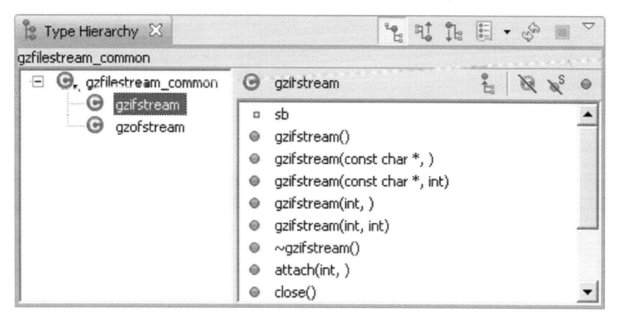

Figure 6.20: Type Hierarchy of a class

This view is similar to *Call Hierarchy* (Section 6.12, on page 79) and *Include Browser* (Section 6.13, on page 81)

Search Type

To search for a type in the project, press *Navigate → Open Type in Hierarchy*. (See *Open Type in Hierarchy* (Figure 6.23, on page 85))

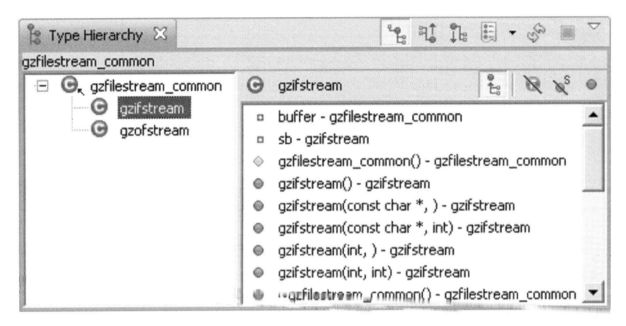

Figure 6.21: Type Hierarchy — with inherited members

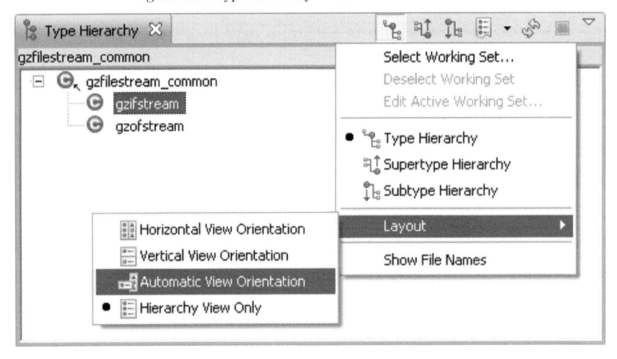

Figure 6.22: Change the Layout of Type Hierarchy View

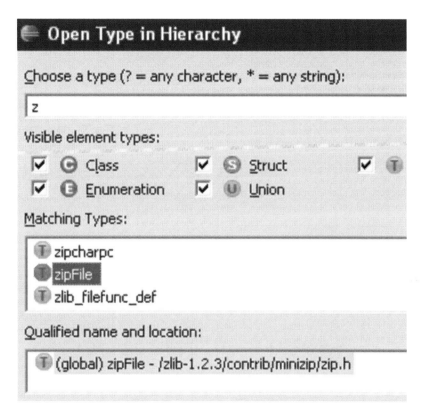

Figure 6.23: Open Type in Hierarchy

Quick Type

To search for a type in the project, press `Ctrl + T`.

6.15 Bookmarks

Bookmark is like *tagging* or *anchoring* a point in your source code where you revert back quickly.

To add a bookmark either press *Edit → Add Bookmark* (OR) Right click on the left editor pane. Click *Add Bookmark*

In Eclipse, it is also possible to *describe* a bookmark. By default the description is the contents of the line. The description can be changed any time. Either during creation of bookmark. Or via the *Bookmark View* (Figure 6.25, on the next page)

We can also see *Bookmarks and the markers in editor* (Figure 6.24, on this page) Hovering on it can also show the description. The left pane shows the anchors points. The right pan shows overview of the complete file.

```
429 {
430     z_stream c_stream; /* compression st
431     int err;
432
433     c_stream.zalloc = (alloc_func)0;
434     c_stream.zfree = (free_func)0;
435     c_stream.opaque = (voidpf)0;
436
437     err = deflateInit(&c_stream, Z_BEST_
438 deflateInit CK_ERR(err, "deflateInit");
439
440     err = deflateSetDictionary(&c_strear
```

Figure 6.24: Bookmarks and the markers in editor

The list of bookmarks can be seen in *Bookmarks View* (Figure 6.25, on the next page). If the view is not visible, activate it using either *Window → Show View → Other → General → Book-*

marks Or quicker keyboard shortcut `Alt + Shift + Q , Q` and then selecting *Bookmarks*

Description ▲	Resource	Path	Location
deflateInit	example.c	/Zlib-1.2.3	line 438
z_stream c_stream; /* compression stream */	example.c	/Zlib-1.2.3	line 430

Figure 6.25: Bookmarks view

Bookmarks can be removed using *Remove Bookmark* entry from *Right click* context menu. Or using the *Bookmarks view* (Figure 6.25, on this page)

We can *Double Click* on *Bookmarks view* (Figure 6.25, on the current page) to jump directly to a bookmark.

We can press `Ctrl + .` and `Ctrl + ,` to navigate to next/previous Bookmark in this file. See *Jumping within the file* (Section 6.8, on page 65) for more.

6.16 Code Formatting

There is a saying - *Code is poetry.* [1] *(But, it depends on the Poet how Beautful that Poem is!)*

The code is written for the compiler. But in long term, programmers have to read that code again and again. C Language is very flexible and *forgiving*. A piece of code that takes seconds for a compiler to interpret may take an eternity [2] for a programmer to understand.

Consider the code example below.

```
void f1() {
  return;
}

int f2()
{ return 0; }

int f3() { return 1; }
```

---

[1] I don't know the original source of that quote; but its tagline of http://wordpress.org.

[2] *Almost* an eternity. If you still don't agree, try to understand the code at The International Obfuscated C Code Contest (http://www.ioccc.org/)

```
int f4(int k)
{
        if (k > 100) {
    return 3; } else k++;
        return k;
}
```

In the above example, f1(), f2(), f3() are written in a separate coding style. Few programmers may have issue with that coding convention. Others may just ignore it. But every one would agree that f4() is written poorly.

```
int f5(int k, int m) {
    if ( k > 100 )
        k++;
        m++;
    if ( m < 100 )
        return --m;
}
```

For that matter, f5() is just killing the C Language. Wrong indentation may force some users to oversee obvious mistakes.

```
int f4(int k) {
    if (k > 100) {
        return 3;
    } else
        k++;
    return k;
}
```

The reformatted f4() looks more understandable. Eclipse can do this kind of *beautification* automatically. Select the code format and just press Ctrl + Shift + F OR *Edit → Format.* Eclipse would automatically fix the formatting.

But the best advantage with Eclipse is that it provides a great control over formatting. This is covered in depth in *Code Style* (Section 8.2, on page 109) in *Editing Code* (Chapter 8, on page 109)

## CHAPTER 7

Building Code

What does Building mean? In C/C++ context, it can be plainly *Compiling* and *Linking*

But it is a little more than that. If a C source file changes, only that file gets compiled. If a C header file changes, every source file that includes it (directly or indirectly) gets compiled.

But, in true context of a build, it is not just *compiling* and *linking*. It normally also involves creating libraries/DLLs/Shared Objects. In larger projects, running static code analysis tools, generating API documentation, running unit tests, code coverage tools can also be part of the build process.

Eclipse can cover all the variations of such builds.

Mainly, Eclipse supports 2 types of *builds*

- *Eclipse Managed Build* (Section 7.1, on the next page)

    - Eclipse manages every thing.

    - Eclipse Gives a GUI to change the paremters/etc.

- *Externally Managed Build* (Section 7.2, on page 101)

    - Eclipse let's other tool do every thing

    - Quite common for *Existing* projects where a build system is already in place.

These are the topics discussed in further detail:

7.1 Eclipse Managed Build

To begin with, this can be the simplest way to build a new Project. (But it only works with GCC and *other* Eclipse supported toolchains.) [1]

CDT gives a GUI to:

- Manage the build

- Selectively exclude/include some files from build.

- Maintain *build configurations* (Section 7.1, on page 94)

- *Indexing* (Section 9.2, on page 132) works out-of-the-box

With Eclipse managed build, Eclipse can automatically create a set of makefiles. These make files can be used with standard make utility. Thus, if the project is managed within Eclipse, developers not using Eclipse can still build the software. It is also useful for automated standalone builds.

Note: Older versions of CDT used to refer this as a *Managed make project*

Creating a sample project

1. Click *File → New → Project*

2. Select C Project

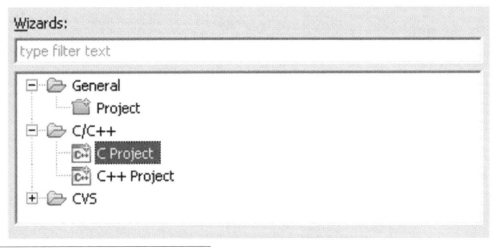

---

[1] Cygwin GCC, Linux GCC, MacOSX GCC, MinGW GCC, Solaris GCC are supported by default. The proprietary distributions based on Eclipse would also support the toolchains of that distribution.

3. Name the project as `Hello World`.

4. Select project type as `Hello World ANSI C Project`

5. Select Tool-chain as `MinGW GCC`

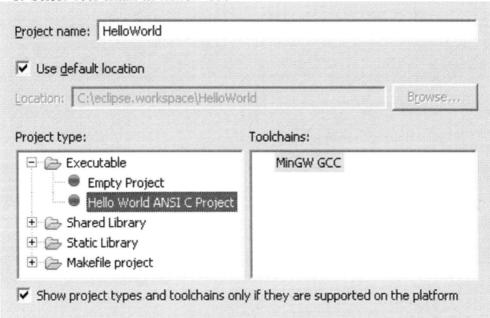

6. Click *Next* button

7. Input your details

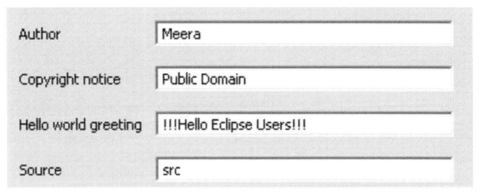

8. Click *Next* button

9. Select *Advanced settings*

10. Select Current builder as *Gnu Make Builder*

11. Click *OK* button

12. Click *Finish* button

13. If you get a message to switch *perspective* (Section 5.8, on page 45), Click Yes

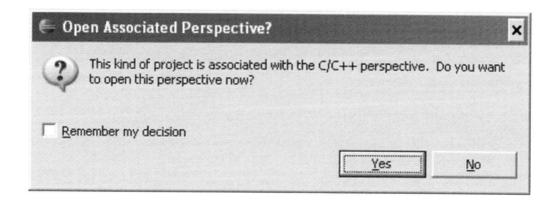

This happens if the previous perspective was not C/C++ perspective.

This is how the *Project Explorer* view would look like.

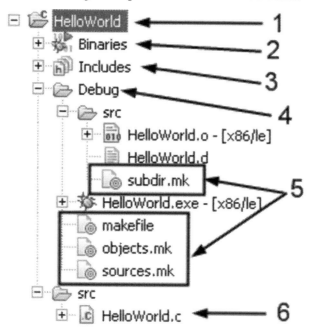

1. The name of the project *HelloWorld*

2. Eclipse would list executables and libraries of the project here.

3. Eclipse would list include directories and header files here.

4. Eclipse generated folder. The name is derived from the build configuration.

5. Eclipse generated Makefiles

6. The actual source file.

To build the project, do either of:

- Press `Ctrl + B`
- Click *Project → Build All*
- Press the *Build Button*

Build Configuration

Build configurations are different ways of building a code. The most basic would be *debug* mode and *retail* mode. In debug mode, the generated objects and executables have debug symbols. For large projects, this can become further complicated. Including files for test code, excluding files for test code, etc.

Each configuration can have unique set of source files, includes, #defines, and other compiler/linker parameters.

Eclipse managed — Externally managed

Eclipse managed make is a good way to begin with.
But in ideal case, projects are pre-existing, with its own set of makefiles/build mechanism. In some cases, fine control over the build is needed. Something that CDT may not be able to give *easily* out of the box. Makefiles may have to be written manually. For such cases, *Externally Managed Build* (Section 7.2, on page 101) has more details.

Changing Build Settings

Eclipse gives control over how the project gets build.

Include / Exclude Files from Build

Use *Right Click → Resource Configuration → Exclude From Build* to add/remove a source file from a *Build Configuration* (Section 7.1, on the current page)

Even finer control can be achieved through, *Project → Properties → C/C++ General → Paths and Symbols → Source Location* (See *Including / Excluding files & directories from build* (Figure 7.1, on the facing page))

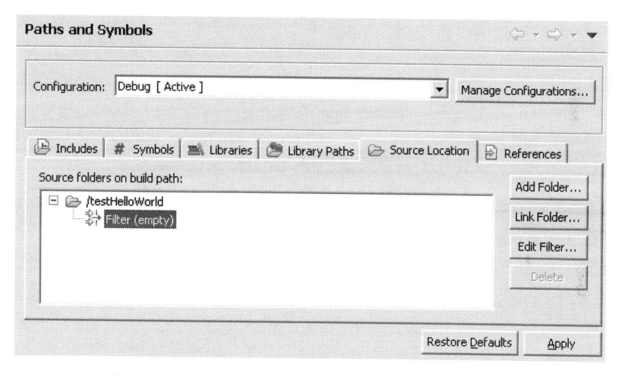

Figure 7.1: Including / Excluding files & directories from build

Compiler Directives

Through *Project → Properties → C/C++ General → Paths and Symbols → Includes* we can *Add include paths to build* (Figure 7.2, on the current page).

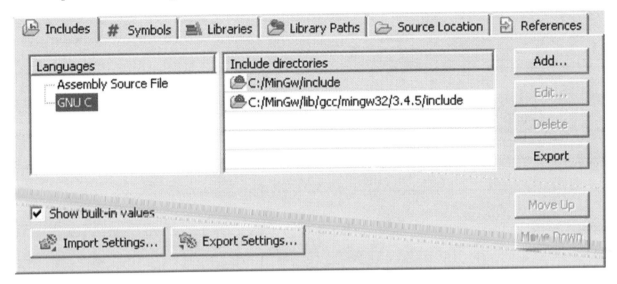

Figure 7.2: Add include paths to build

Through *Project → Properties → C/C++ General → Paths and Symbols → Symbols* we can *Add compiler defines to build* (Figure 7.3, on the facing page).

Change the Make Utility

To *Change the default build utility* (Figure 7.4, on the next page), from `make` to something else, go to *Project → Properties → C/C++ Build → Builder Settings*

To change *Advanced build settings* (Figure 7.5, on page 98) , e.g. using Parallel jobs for build (-j), or build on every save, go to *Project → Properties → C/C++ Build → Behaviour*

Advanced toolchain specific settings

The toolchain can be selected form *Project → Settings → C/C++ Build → Tool Chain Editor*.

To *Change general settings of the Tool-Chain* (Figure 7.6, on page 99), like, enable warnings (`-Wall`), don't include standard system header files during compilation (`-nostdinc`), etc. go to *Project → Settings → C/C++ Build → Settings → Tool Settings*

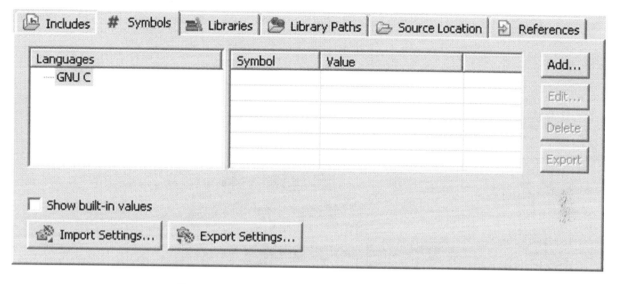

Figure 7.3: Add compiler defines to build

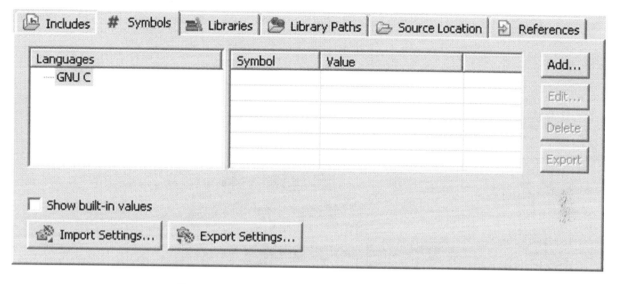

Figure 7.4: Change the default build utility

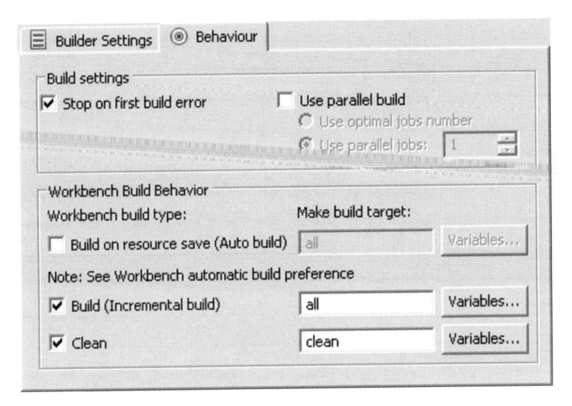

Figure 7.5: Advanced build settings

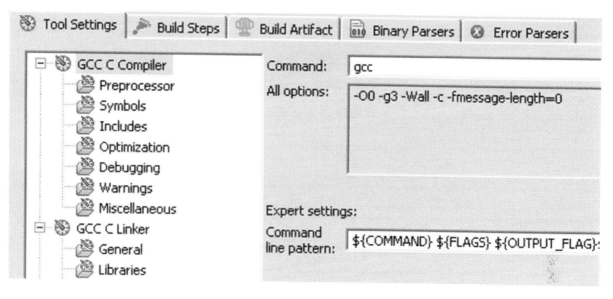

Figure 7.6: Change general settings of the Tool-Chain

We can also *Change the build artifacts (dll/lib/exe)* (Figure 7.7, on this page). We can control if we want to build a DLL/Shared Object, static library, or an executable out of this project.

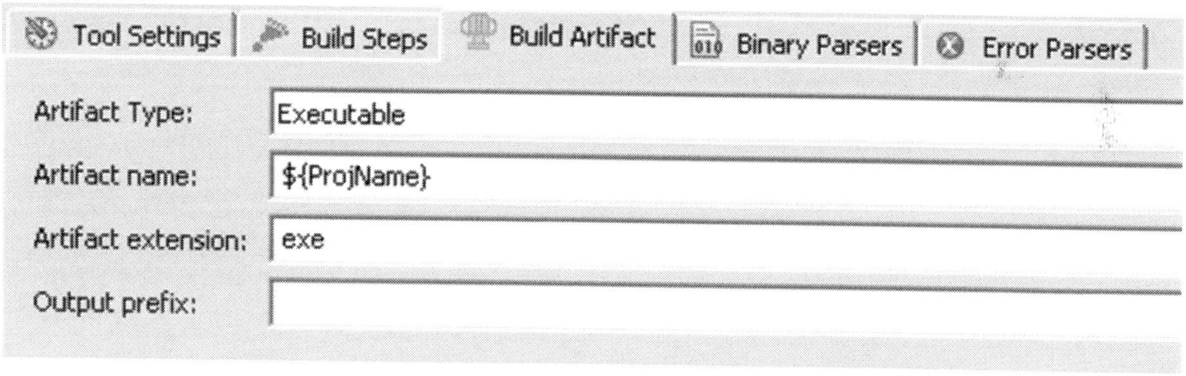

Figure 7.7: Change the build artifacts (dll/lib/exe)

Pre-Build and Post-Build Steps

To *Add pre-build and post-build steps* (Figure 7.8, on the next page), go to *Project → Settings → C/C++ Build → Settings → Build Steps*

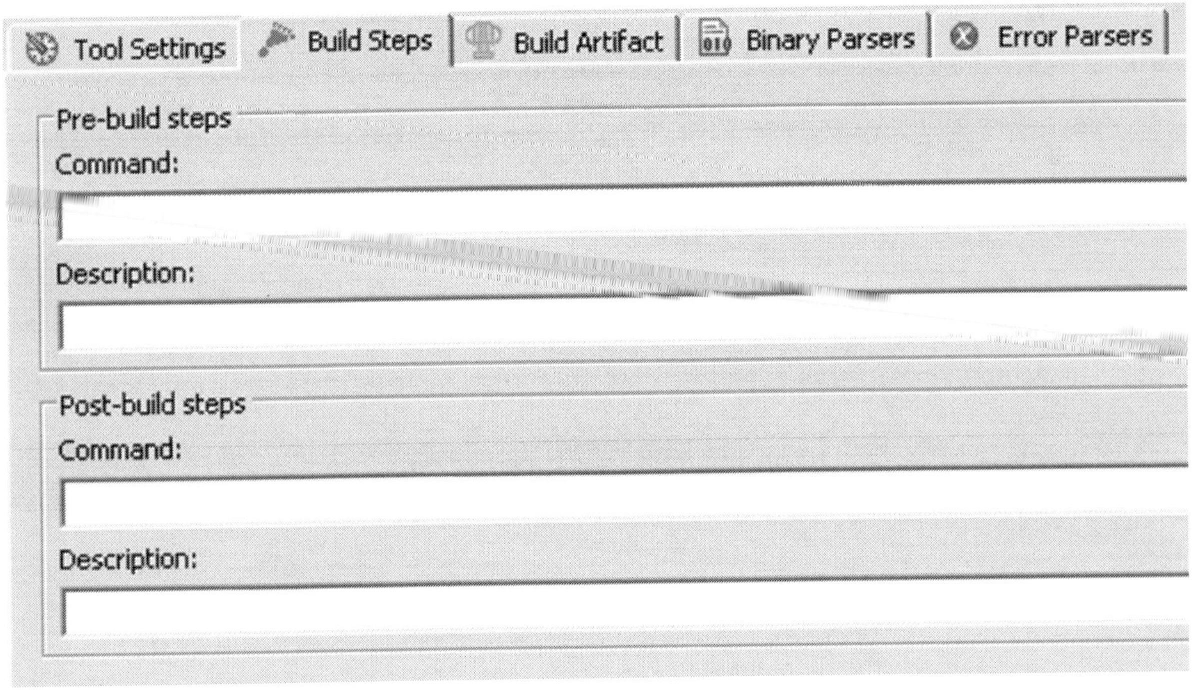

Figure 7.8: Add pre-build and post-build steps

7.2 Externally Managed Build

Build systems *not* managed by Eclipse.

- Recommended (needed) for existing projects.
- Any build system that supports command line build can be covered using this mechanism. (e.g. *Using MSVC* (Section 7.4, on page 107))

It involves these steps:

1. Add the source within Eclipse
2. Tell Eclipse how to build it.
3. (Optionally) Fix *Indexing* (Section 9.2, on page 132)

Since we are covering Zlib source in this book, let's have a walk through how that code is imported / built into Eclipse.

Tip: For our example, Zlib is present in `C:\sw\src\zlib\1.2.3\zlib-1.2.3`

And the build commands is

```
make -f win32/Makefile.gcc LOC="-DDEBUG -g" all
```

Follow the steps as shown below to import *any Makefile based* project into Eclipse.

The parameters in steps marked `[X]` might have to be adapted other projects.

---

1. Create a new C Project. *File* → *New* →*Project*, `C Project` *(Select* `C++ Project` *if your project is based on C++')*
2. `[X]` Set project name as `Zlib-1.2.3`
3. Unset *Use default location*
4. `[X]` Set *Location* as `C:\sw\src\zlib\1.2.3\zlib-1.2.3`
5. Set *Project Type* as *Makefile project* → *Empty Project*
6. Set *Toolchain* as *MinGW GCC* (On Linux, select *Linux GCC*)

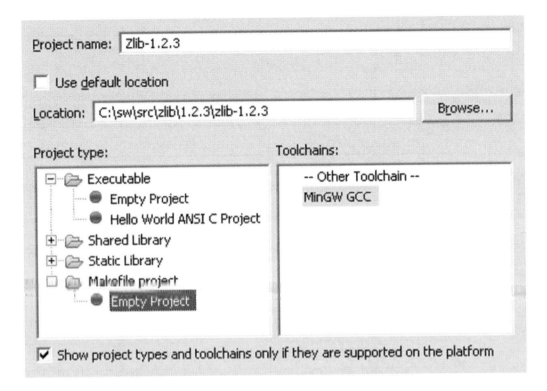

7. Click *Next* button

8. Click *Advanced Settings*

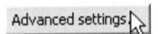

9. Select the option, *C/C++ Build*

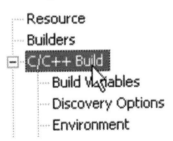

10. Change the build command to

```
make -f win32/Makefile.gcc LOC="-DDEBUG -g"
```

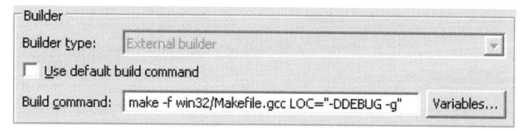

11. The *Console* view should show the build output.

```
Console  ⊠
C-Build [Zlib-1.2.3]

**** Build of configuration Default for project Zlib-1.2.3 ****

make -f win32/Makefile.gcc LOC=-DDEBUG -g all
gcc -DDEBUG -g -O3 -Wall -c -o adler32.o adler32.c
gcc -DDEBUG -g -O3 -Wall -c -o compress.o compress.c
```

12. The *Project Explorer* view should show the generated binaries.

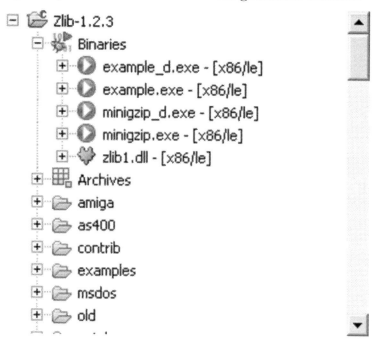

Settings for Externally managed build

The feature to *Change the Make Utility* (Section 7.1, on page 96) is already described.

7.3 Remote Building

Sounds absurd! Why would one edit files on one machine, and compile on another? But there is a niche for such kind of activity. The biggest reason being the presence of compiler on host/target machine.

Assuming, you have a setup where compilation takes place on a remote machine, say Linux, but you want to edit your source code in Windows. Can Eclipse Help? How much?

This *big* issue can be broken into three parts.

1. (Always) Sync source code from Windows and Linux before build

2. Trigger build from Windows to Linux

   These include

   - make all

   - make clean

3. Sync output paths (Linux to Windows) so that Eclipse can take you to correct location for compiler warnings and errors.

Note: Instead of just speaking of theories, we will see actually happen on a live project here. For this particular use case, we are building A QT based (http://code.google.com/p/gtest-runner-qt/) from Windows 7 machine on Ubuntu Linux.

Sync source code

The simplest possible solution would be to use samba on Linux, and mount the shared folder in Windows. Let Windows access that folder

Note: If samba share is not an alternative, setup a script to sync the source code. Make it part of batch script we write in *Trigger Build* (Section 7.3, on the next page).

Obviously, you would like your current source code in Windows environment to be compiled in linux. For this, you will have to use rsync or scp or such other unix powertool of samba share is not an option.

Trigger Build

1. Write a `Windows` batch file to trigger remote build.

   e.g.

   ```
   C:\opt\plink.exe -ssh -l dehlia 192.168.0.101 -pw SoSecret \
   -t "bash;cd /home/dehlia/dev/gtest-runner-qt.dev; make %*"
   ```

   Save this file to an appropriate location.

   (Change the path and host name as appropriate; The above command is split in multiple lines. Please see PLink (http://the.earth.li/ sgtatham/putty/0.60/-htmldoc/Chapter7.html#plink) manual for more information.)

   > **Warning:** The current setup is using plain-cleartext password. If you do not want to do that use Passwordless login feature of Putty (http://the.earth.li/-sgtatham/putty/0.60/htmldoc/Chapter8.html#pubkey)

2. Update Eclipse build command in *Project → Properties → C/C++ Build*.

   (a) Set *Builder Settings → Builder → Build Command* to **cmd /c remote_build.bat**

   (b) Set *Build location → Build directory* to the directory where this batch file is kept.

Handle output paths

1. Create an *Empty* C/C++ Project.

2. Imitate the reference directory structure in the project

   e.g. In our case, we are imitating:

   ```
   /usr/include/qt4/QtCore/
   ```

   `QtCore` is a `link` to another mounted location from linux tree.

3. Link the development project (**) to *Empty* project.

   Go to *Project → Properties → Project References* and select the *Empty* project.

Tune Error Parser (Optional)

1. Go to *Project → Properties → C/C++ Build → Settigns → Error Parsers*

2. Select the compiler/compiler family being used by you.

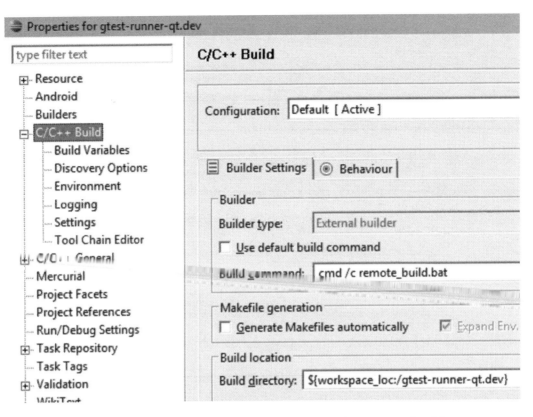

Figure 7.9: Set Eclipse Project properties for remote build.

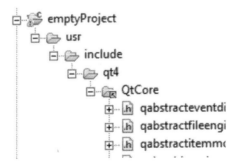

Figure 7.10: Imitate a linux directory tree in windows

Good to Go!

This setup *worked* for me, but I cannot simply say *Works For Me*.

Did you find any issues/problems with the current explanation *Contact Me* (Appendix J, on page 178).

42 errors, 0 warnings, 38 others			
Description ▲	Resource	Path	Location
⊗ no match for â€˜operator<<â€™ in â	GTestParser.cpp	/gtest-runner-qt.dev/src	line 77
⊗ no match for â€˜operator<<â€™ in â	GTestParser.cpp	/gtest-runner-qt.dev/src	line 82
⊗ no matching function for call to â€˜(	GTestSuite.cpp	/gtest-runner-qt.dev/src	line 95
⊗ template argument 2 is invalid	TestTreeModel.cpp	/gtest-runner-qt.dev/src	line 269
⊗ template argument 2 is invalid	TestTreeModel.h	/gtest-runner-qt.dev/include	line 54
⊟ i Infos (38 items)			
i QDataStream& operator<<	qbytearray.h	/emptyProject/usr/include/qt4/QtCore	line 570
i QDataStream& operator<<	qchar.h	/emptyProject/usr/include/qt4/QtCore	line 391
i QDataStream& operator<<	qregexp.h	/emptyProject/usr/include/qt4/QtCore	line 143
i QDataStream& operator<<	qstring.h	/emptyProject/usr/include/qt4/QtCore	line 1027
i QDataStream& operator<<	qstringlist.h	/emptyProject/usr/include/qt4/QtCore	line 230

Figure 7.11: Warnings and errors of remote build.

7.4 Using MSVC

Note: It is not possible to debug MSVC based projects inside Eclipse

MSVC (Appendix A, on page 162) supports command line interface (devenv) to build software. This makes it possible to build those projects inside Eclipse.

For a solution file called `Solution.sln` and Project `MyCppProject`, the build command is:

```
devenv Solution.sln /project MyCppProject /build /nologo
```

Create a batch file as shown below (and make changes as needed)

```
IF NOT DEFINED VSINSTALLDIR (
    IF DEFINED VS80COMNTOOLS (
        CALL "%VS80COMNTOOLS%VCVARS32.BAT"
    ) ELSE (
        IF DEFINED VS71COMNTOOLS (
            CALL "%VS71COMNTOOLS%vsvars32.bat"
```

```
            )
        )
    )
IF NOT DEFINED VSINSTALLDIR (
    @ECHO ###%~0###ERROR Setting Up environment.. ###
)

@REM  TODO: Change to the path of your project
cd /d D:\Path\To\My\Project

@REM  TODO: Change to name of solution and project
devenv Solution.sln /project MyCppProject /build /nologo
```

Use this batch file as build utility in *Change the Make Utility* (Section 7.1, on page 96)

Note: *Contact* (Appendix J, on page 178) the author if you need some help in setting up MOVC or builder inside Eclipse.

Note: For some common steps, that are not part of normal build process, Eclipse also has a feature to add *External Tools* (Section 9.1, on page 131).

## CHAPTER 8

Editing Code

8.1 Text Editor

There are *unfair* comparison of Eclipse with other *text editors*. [1] But Eclipse is an *IDE*. Eclipse *has a* text editor. It's a different Text Editor. There cannot be a 1:1 mapping between all the features of Eclipse and other text editors. But still Eclipse is feature rich.

Here are some of the keyboard shortcuts within Eclipse.

Action	Key
Delete Line	`Ctrl + D`
Delete to End of Line	`Ctrl + Shift + Delete`
Delete Next / Previous Word	`Ctrl + Delete` / `Ctrl + Backspace`
Insert blank line Below Current Line	`Shift + Enter`
Insert blank line Above Current Line	`Ctrl + Shift + Enter`
Join Lines	`Ctrl + Alt + J`
Move Line(s) Up / Down	`Alt + Down` / `Alt + Up`
Copy Lines Up	`Ctrl + Alt + Up`
Copy Lines Down	`Ctrl + Alt + Down`
Scroll Up / Down	`Ctrl + Down` / `Ctrl + Up`
Maximize - Minimize	`Ctrl + M`

8.2 Code Style

---

[1] Vim, Notepad

Note: This chapter is a continuation of *Code Formatting* (Section 6.16, on page 87)

Tabs or Spaces? Or Both? Indent with 2 spaces? 3? 4? Or 8 spaces? Do these questions make any sense to you? If yes, you would be lucky to have Eclipse. If not — pity on your peer developers.

Most open source projects have their own *strict* coding conventions. [2] The feature of *Code Style* within Eclipse can make this task very easy for developers. Eclipse also supports *profiles* for using different coding styles. (Or share code style within in Organization.)

Profiles

A profile is a set of rules for Code Style/formatting.

By default, Eclipse has the following profiles.

- GNU
- K&R
- BSD/Allman
- Whitesmits

You can also create/share your own profile. For e.g. let's take [BSD/Allman] profile, and extend it.

Go to *Window → Preferences → C/C++ → Code Style*. You will get a list of *Code style profiles* (Figure 8.1, on the facing page)

Click on New and select the base profile. (Figure 8.2, on the next page)

Extend the profile (Figure 8.3, on page 112) and save it. Now we have profile `Meera` that is almost same as `BSD/Allman` but uses SPACES instead of TABS.

You can see the effect of your settings in the right area of *the dialogue box.* (Figure 8.3, on page 112) This will give you a hint on changing the style. The Eclipse code style formatter is much more extendible.

Share/Export/Import Profiles

The profiles can be shared across projects/developers.

---

[2] Linux kernel (http://kerneltrap.org/mailarchive/git/2007/10/16/344968) mandates 8 spaces of indentation.

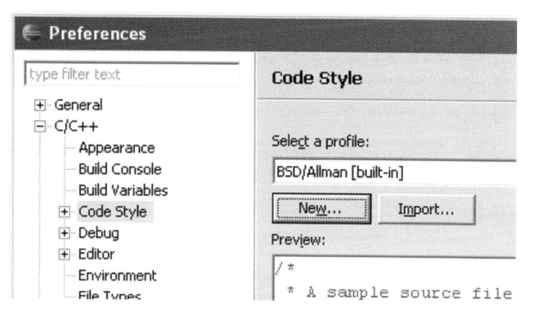

Figure 8.1: Code style profiles

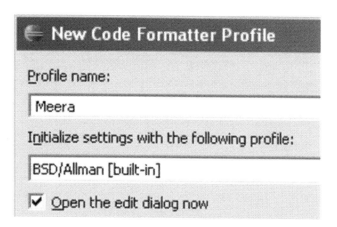

Figure 8.2: New Code Style

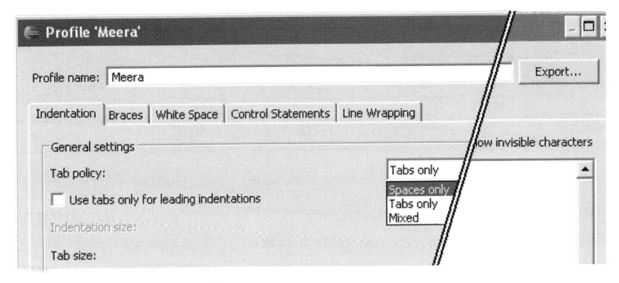

Figure 8.3. Editing Code Style

To export code profile, use the Export in *Editing Code Style* (Figure 8.3, on this page) dialogue. To import, use the Import in *Code style profiles* (Figure 8.1, on page 111) of a Project [3] or Workspace [4].

8.3 Local History

Eclipse automatically keeps track of the changes. Changes made few days ago... a few minutes ago. This is stored in a *Local History*. The changes are stored automatically.

You can control how long you want to keep the changes. And how many changes you want Eclipse to remember. The default preferences for this can be set from *Window → Preferences → General → Workspace → Local History*. These are the preferences that can be modified:

- Date to keep files
- Maximum entries per file
- Maximum file size (MB)

How to use the local history? You can either compare your source file with local history, or replace it altogether. *Right Click* on the source file to access the context sensitive menu:

- *Compare With → Local History*

---

[3] *Project → Properties → C/C++ General → Code Style.*
[4] *Window → Preferences → C/C++ → Code Style*

- *Replace With* → *Local History*
- *Replace With* → *Previous from Local History*

Let's change `example.c` to see this in action. *Right click* on `example.c`. Select *Compare With* → *Local History*

You will get *Local History View* (Figure 8.4, on this page). You can see the original file by double clicking on the file. To see the difference against current file, *enable compare mode.* (Figure 8.5, on the next page) You can also group revisions by date. Once compare mode is enabled, double click on an entry in *Local History View* (Figure 8.4, on this page). A *sample diff* (Figure 8.6, on the next page) is shown. (See that Eclipse diff is intelligent to find that all changes are only to `comparessBound` function.

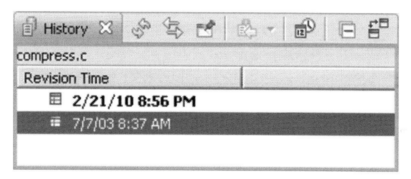

Figure 8.4: Local History View

8.4 Code Completion

Code completion is one of the most basic features of a language sensitive IDE. Press `Ctrl + Space` and Eclipse would be of immediate help.

But Eclipse takes it one step further.

Pressing `f` and then `Ctrl + Space` brings in window for completion.

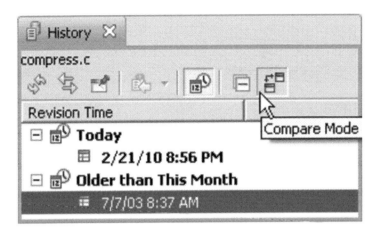

Figure 8.5: Enable Compare mode in local history

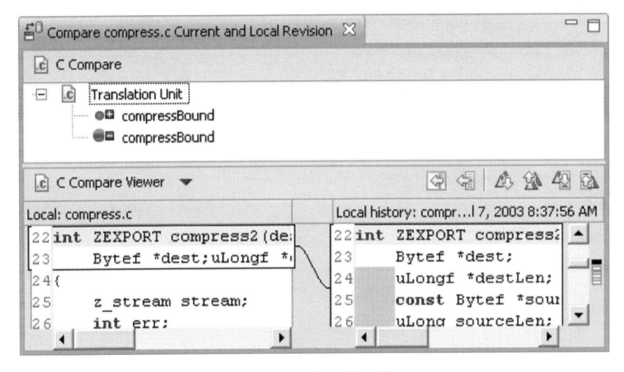

Figure 8.6: Sample Diff

```
test_deflate(compr, comprLen);
test_inflate(compr, comprLen, uncompr, unco
```

```
f
```
t	● fclose(FILE *) : int ▲
t	● fclose_file_func(voidpf opaque,voidpf stream) , uncompr
	● fcvt(double,int,int *,int *) : char * , uncompr
t	● fdopen(int,const char *) : FILE *
t	● feof(FILE *) : int
c	● ferror(FILE *) : int , uncompr
	● ferror_file_func(voidpf opaque,voidpf stream)

Pressing Ctrl + Space again cycles through types of completions. In this case its for *Code Templates* (Section 8.5, on the following page).

```
f
```
	▣ for - for loop	**for** (var = 0; var
t	▣ for - for loop with temporary variable	
t		}
r		

Pressing . , -> and :: also activates content assist automatically. This behavior can be configured via *Window → Preferences → C/C++ → Editor → Content Assist*

Word Completion

Word completions takes context sensitivity one step backward. (Or maybe forward.) It does not depend on context sensitive information. Pressing Alt + / would complete current word. The most important usage would be within comments. Where in you may want to explain about some functions/variables. The function name would not be context sensitive within the comment region but the word would still complete itself.

8.5 Code Templates

Many times the type of code written is *repetitive*. (If you don't agree, you have not yet heard about design patterns.) Eclipse support many kinds of templates. Higher level templates for files/function. Lower level templates for loops and similar constructs. You can even have your own custom templates.

What makes these templates special, their own inherent intelligence.

e.g. The *for loop* template:

```
for (${var} = 0; ${var} < ${max}; ++${var}) {
    ${line_selection}${cursor}
}
```

When a *for* template is created, you need to enter the *var* only once. The other two entries (comparison and increment) are filled automatically.

Sample — For Loop

Here is an example to introduce for loop over a selection of code.

1. Select the code block

```
11      out.close();
12
13      izstream in("temp.gz"); // read it back
14      char *x = read_string(in), *y = new char[2
15      in > y > z;
16      in.close();
17      cout << x << endl << y << endl << z << en
18
19      out.open("temp.gz"); // try ascii output;
```

2. Press Ctrl + Space. Eclipse would also show a preview of the changes

```
11        out.close();
12
13    izstream in("temp.gz"); // read it back
14  ⊟ do - do while statement          ▲  for (int var = 0; var < max; ++var) {
15  ⊟ for - for loop                    ▬       izstream in("temp.gz"); // read it back
16  ▣ for - for loop with temporary variable      char *x = read_string(in), *y = new char
17  ⊟ if - if statement                         in > y > z;
18  ⊟ try - try catch block                      in.close();
19  ● g : char *                                 cout << x << endl << y << endl << z << e
20  ● h : char []                        )
21  ● out : ozstream
```

3. Eclipse has now put in the template. Note that colored blocks and the cursor mark (Circled for reference)

```
11        out.close();
12
13⊖    for (int var = 0; var < max; ++var) {
14          izstream in("temp.gz"); // read it back
15          char *x = read_string(in), *y = new char[256], z[256];
16          in > y > z;
17          in.close();
18          cout << x << endl << y << endl << z << endl;
19        }
20
21      out.open("temp.gz"); // try ascii output; zcat temp.gz to see
```

4. Type the value for the iterator. (In this case iTest and press TAB

```
11        out.close();
12
13⊖    for (int iTest = 0; iTest < max; ++iTest) {
14          izstream in("temp.gz"); // read it back
15          char *x = read_string(in), *y = new char[25
16          in > y > z;
17          in.close();
18          cout << x << endl << y << endl << z << endl
19        }
20
21      out.open("temp.gz"); // try ascii output; zcat
```

5. Now you can update value of the MAX limit.

```
11          out.close();
12
13⊖     for (int iTest = 0; iTest < iMAX; ++iTest) {
14          izstream in("temp.gz"); // read it back
15          char *x = read_string(in), *y = new char[25
16          in > y > z;
17          in.close();
18          cout << x << endl << y << endl << z << endl
19      }
20
21      out.open("temp.gz"); // try ascii output; zcat
```

8.6 Change Markers

Before saving file, it is a good reference to see what parts of file have changed. Or when Eclipse is asked to do *Auto Formatting* (Section 8.2, on page 109) or Use *Code Templates* (Section 8.5, on page 116), we need to know which lines have changed.

As shown in *Sample — For Loop* (Section 8.5, on page 116), once the for loop is auto inserted, the left side of the editor that shows line numbers is colored.

Press Ctrl + Shift + Q to enable/disable this feature. (Or *Window* → *Preferences* → *General* → *Editors* → *Text Editors* → *Quick Diff* → *Enable quick diff*)

From the *Quick diff preferences* (Figure 8.7, on the facing page), you can enable to have the overview in the right column. Or change the colors. (Or have quick diff against supported configuration management system.) The *Quick diff accessibility preferences* (Figure 8.8, on the next page) can enable usage of characters to mark change.

8.7 Smart Insert

It is a set of minor *assistance* that Eclipse provides. But over all, makes a huge difference in longer run. What does this mode do? Auto insert matching ", ', (, [, < and {. When copy-pasting code — take care of correct indentation in destination.

To enabled/disable this mode: Ctrl + Shift + Insert OR *Edit* → *Smart Insert Mode*

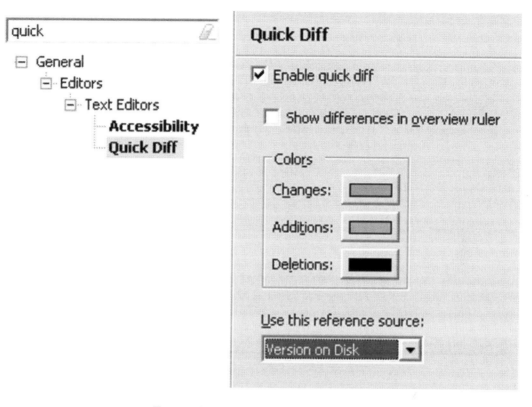

Figure 8.7: Quick diff preferences

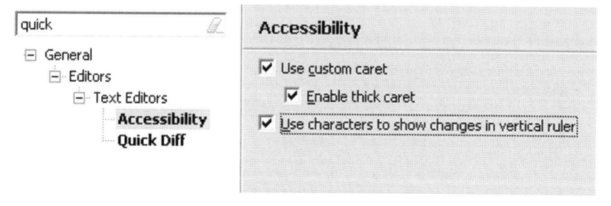

Figure 8.8: Quick diff accessibility preferences

To customize the preferences: *Window → Preferences → C/C++ → Editor → Typing*

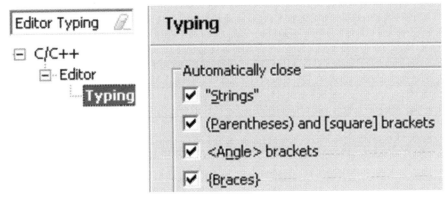

- Strings - When you press one " (quote) , the 2nd " (quote) is automatically inserted.
- Similar controls are available for (,), [,], ‹ ›, {, }

The interesting part is, if you *manually* press the *second* closing quote/bracket, it is overwritten.

8.8 Refactoring

What is refactoring? In simple words, it is just renaming of identifiers [5]. It is about changing the source code such that that there is no functional change in program's behaviour. More can be read at http://en.wikipedia.org/wiki/Code_refactoring

Rename

The most basic application of refactoring is to rename a C/C++ identifier [1]. This renaming is context sensitive. Eclipse knows whether you are renaming something globally or locally. Just select the identifier and press Ctrl + Shift + R. The advantage over renaming? See an example. The file example.c has c_stream in almost every function. If we *refactor* c_stream to cmprStream in test_deflate, the *rename* would happen only in test_deflate. c_stream would remain as it is in other function.

Here is refactoring/renaming in action. Select c_stream and press Ctrl + Shift + R (Or *Refactor → Rename*). A *dialog would pop up* (Figure 8.9, on the facing page). Enter the new name and press Preview. Eclipse would show *Diff of the proposed changes* (Figure 8.10, on the next page). Here is a preview of *c_stream replaced with cmprStream* (Figure 8.11, on the facing page)

---

[5] Functions, variables, typedefs, enumerators, defines, etc.

Figure 8.9: Rename c_stream to cmprStream

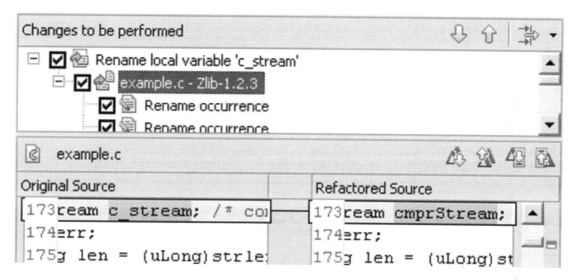

Figure 8.10: Diff of the proposed changes

```
175        uLong len = (uLong)strlen(hello)+1;
176
177        c_stream.zal                177        cmprStream.zalloc = (alloc_func)0;
178        c_stream.zfr                178        cmprStream.zfree  = (free_func)0;
179        c_stream.opa                179        cmprStream.opaque = (voidpf)0;
180                                    180
181        err = deflat                181        err = deflateInit(&cmprStream, Z_DEFAULT_COMPRESS
182        CHECK_ERR(er                182        CHECK_ERR(err, "deflateInit");
183                                    183
184        c_stream.nex                184        cmprStream.next_in  = (Bytef*)hello;
185        c_stream.nex                185        cmprStream.next_out = compr;
186
```

Figure 8.11: c_stream replaced with cmprStream

(The best use of refactoring this way is to rename local variables `foo`, `bar` and the omnipresent `int i=0` in loops)

Extract Local Variable

Complex operations are difficult to read. If they are reduced with intermediate local variables, code becomes more readable. Eclipse can help to do that.

1. Select the expression

```
void test()
{
    int i = 10, j = 10, k = 10;

    k += i + j;
}
```

2. Press `Ctrl + Shift + L` (Or *Refactor → Extract Local Variable*). Key in the local variable name (in this case `i_plus_j`)

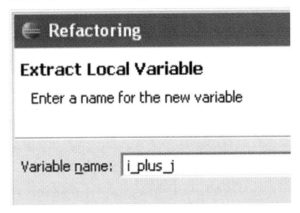

3. Eclipse would replace the variable name.

```
void test()
{
    int i = 10, j = 10, k = 10;
    int i_plus_j = i + j;
    k += i_plus_j;
}
```

Extract Constants / Magic Numbers

Magic numbers are easy to write, and difficult to interpret later. Better replace with better meaning. Eclipse can help to do this, too.

1. Select the constant you want to replace. (In this case 10)

```
void test()
{
    int i = 10, j = 10, k = 10;
    int i_plus_j = i + j;
    k += i_plus_j;
}
```

2. Press Alt + C (Or *Refactor → Extract Constant*). Key in the new constant name (in this case TEN)

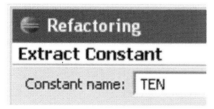

3. Eclipse would replace all the 10/ s with TEN/ s

```
void test()
{
    int i = TEN, j = TEN, k = TEN;
    int i_plus_j = i + j;
    k += i_plus_j;
}
```

Extract Functions

We can reduce a set of source lines to a meaningful function. It is not just copy/pasting code from one place to another. In some cases *necessary* local variables have to be passed in. Either by reference in CPP, or using pointers in C. Eclipse is intelligent enough to figure out the necessary local variables to be passed in. And also can figure out if they have to be passed using reference, pointers or just by value.

1. Select the source lines you want to extract as function.

```
void test()
{
    int i = TEN, j = TEN, k = TEN;
    int i_plus_j = i + j;
    k += i_plus_j;
}
```

2. Press Alt + Shift + M (Or *Refactor → Extract Function*). Key in the function name.

Function Name

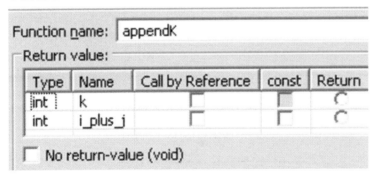

Function name: appendK

Return value:

Type	Name	Call by Reference	const	Return
int	k			○
int	i_plus_j			○

☐ No return-value (void)

3. Eclipse would replace the source lines with a function call.

```
int appendK(int k, int i_plus_j)
{
  k += i_plus_j;
  return k;
}

void test()
{
    int i = TEN, j = TEN, k = TEN;
    int i_plus_j = i + j;
    k = appendK(k, i_plus_j);
}
```

But, every selected source lines cannot be extracted to a function. We can not extract lines with `return` or `break`.

8.9 Task Tags

Eclipse can automatically list the TODOs and FIXMEs from the source code.

	!	Description	Resource	Path	Location	Type
☑	⬇	Refactor/split the source file logically			Unknown	Task
	‼	FIXME That thing	testHelloWorld.c	/testHelloWorld/src	line 12	C/C++ Task
	‼	TODO Meera normal for others. High for me.	testHelloWorld.c	/testHelloWorld/src	line 16	C/C++ Task
		TODO add more documentation	testHelloWorld.c	/testHelloWorld/src	line 27	C/C++ Task
	⬇	XXX change the copyright header	testHelloWorld.c	/testHelloWorld/src	line 10	C/C++ Task
	⬇	XXX Something not so important	testHelloWorld.c	/testHelloWorld/src	line 14	C/C++ Task

Using *Prefences → C/C++ → Task Tags* you can change the priority of a tag.

Personal Task Tags

If the TODOs and FIXMEs are *religiously* used, monitored and fixed within your project, a good usage can be of Personal Task Tags.

You can add a new Task Tag, e.g. We add TODO Meera in *Prefences → C/C++ → Task Tags*. We add it as a high priority tag. This way, we can show a task with high priority for us, while with a normal priority for other users.

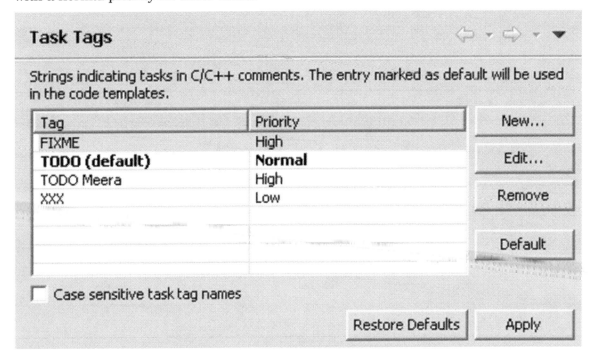

8.10 Display Layouts

The look and feel of Eclipse can be changed. You only need to drag and drop. Drop to the new location you want. The layout can be made the way you prefer. The possibilities are limitless.

Side By Side

Just to give an example, here we are showing Editor being put side by side.

1. Drag the editor tab to the new location

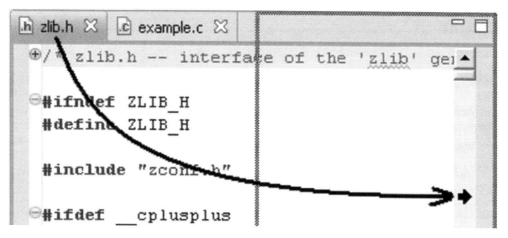

2. Once the tab is dropped, editor is side by side

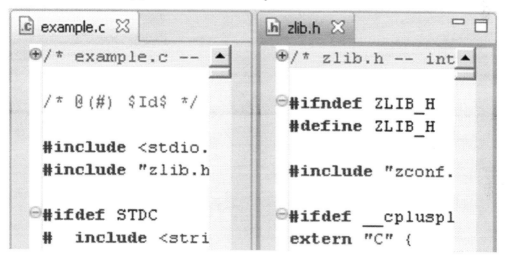

The same way, we have up/down, etc. Even multiple views. Its all for the developer's convenience.

See a new Views

Assuming we want to see a new view. (In this case, Bookmarks view)

1. Press *Window → Show View → Other* (Or Alt + Shift + Q, Q

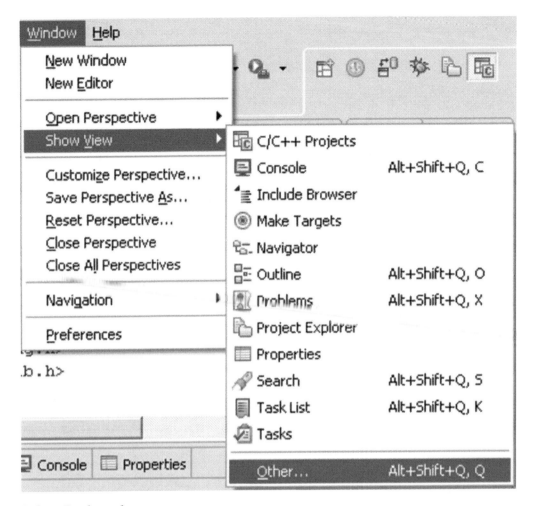

2. Select Bookmarks

3. You will get *Bookmarks view* (Figure 6.25, on page 87) within workspace.

You can place it where-ever you want, just drag and drop as we did to *place editors side-by-side* (Section 8.10, on page 126).

(In a similar way, you can add any View you want.)

Maximized / Minimized

Each view can be maximized. Double click on Stack, or press the maximize button, or `Ctrl + M`. Once maximized, other views get *Trimmed* around. Here is an image showing that operation in action.

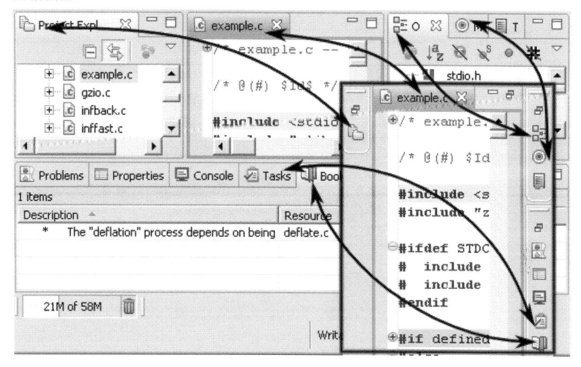

Save the Layout

If you like the layout, and would like to use it often in future, save it. Just press *Window → Save Perspective As*.

Reset the Layout

The changes can be reverted back any time. Just press *Window → Reset Perspective*

8.11 White Spaces

The worst hidden thing that can silently happen to a code is a Mix of tabs and spaces. Choose one of them in your code practice, but not both!

Window → *Preferences* → *General* → *Editors* → *Text Editors* has the relevant choices.

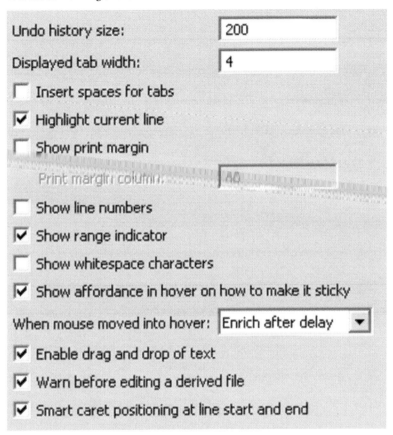

The choices are self explanatory.

If you want to quickly enable/disable show white-space, press 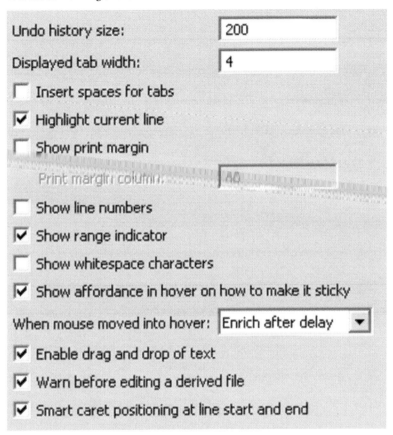 in the toolbar.

## CHAPTER 9

Tweaking Eclipse/CDT

Eclipse/CDT is intelligent enough to figure out standard settings [1] in ideal case [2]. But if you have to use build system that Eclipse/CDT does not understand out-of-the-box, human intervention is needed. This section is dedicated to those settings.

9.1 External Tools

Sample use of this feature can be to

- Generating API Docs via Doxygen
- Running Lint tools
- Translating XML files to API Docs and API header files
- Uploading binaries to test server

From in the tool bar, you can add new external tool.

Note: This chapter is still under construction. *Contact* (Appendix J, on page 178) the author if you need some help.

---

[1] Compiler options (#defines), Include paths.
[2] Using GNU Make, gcc compiler.

9.2 Indexing

What is indexing?

If you already have heard of CTAGS, ETAGS, etc. you already know what an indexer is. A search engine, e.g. Google, is also an indexer. Basically, indexing just makes search and lookup faster.

For C/C++ language, the indexer makes navigating through code faster. But, indexing is not just about navigating thought the code faster. It is also about correctly interpreting code.

If there are some issues with Indexing, we will see editor view like this.

Figure 9.1: Error in indexing

To fix this issue, we will have to tell Eclipse how to parse the C File.

Go to *Project Properties → C/C++ General → Paths and Symbols*. You should get *Add Includes Dialogue* (Figure 9.2, on the facing page) Click Add button.

Then *Add required path to fix indexing* (Figure 9.3, on the next page). After adding, you should see *See the list of include paths* (Figure 9.4, on page 134).

If everything goes well, we should be able to see *Editor view with Indexing fixed* (Figure 9.5, on page 134). If it *does not* go well, *Create a parser log for advanced diagnostics* (Figure 9.6, on page 134). We can then see *Diagnostic information in indexing parser* (Figure 9.7, on page 135)

If you still have indexing errors, you may have to add Compiler Preprocessor Defines in *# Symbols* in the tab next to *Add Includes Dialogue* (Figure 9.2, on the facing page)

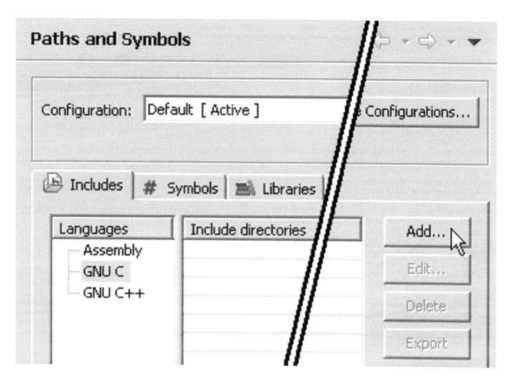

Figure 9.2: Add Includes Dialogue

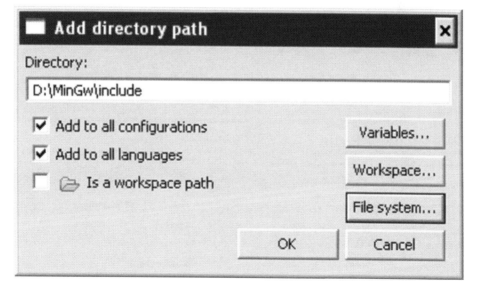

Figure 9.3: Add required path to fix indexing

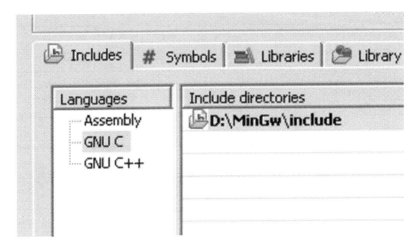

Figure 9.4: See the list of include paths

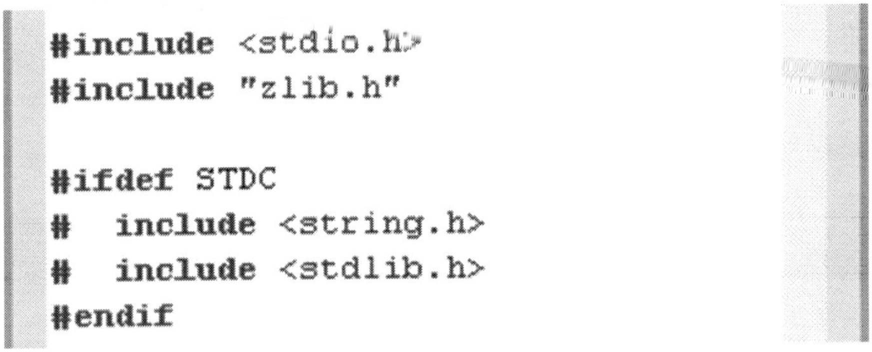

```
#include <stdio.h>
#include "zlib.h"

#ifdef STDC
#   include <string.h>
#   include <stdlib.h>
#endif
```

Figure 9.5: Editor view with Indexing fixed

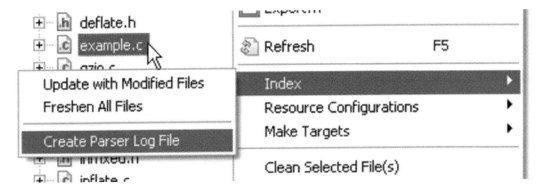

Figure 9.6: Create a parser log for advanced diagnostics

```
Scanner problems:
    Unresolved inclusion: <stdio.h> in file:
    Unresolved inclusion: <string.h> in file:
    Unresolved inclusion: <stdlib.h> in file:


Parser problems:


Unresolved names:
    Attempt to use symbol failed: stderr in f
```

Figure 9.7: Diagnostic information in indexing parser

CDT/Indexer

The C Language Indexer with CDT also does the same thing as CTAGS/ETAGS. It first scans throughout the source code. Derives information related to C/C++ Language. Builds up a knowledge bank, an INDEX. This index makes many features quick and possible. e.g. *Quick Preview* (Section 6.6, on page 60), and *Jumping to Declaration/Definition* (Section 6.9, on page 68) is not possible without such index. The indexer reads the source code, parses it, and creates a quick knowledge bank. Using this knowledge bank, Eclipse can jump around references in the project easily and quickly.

Note: Indexing is a *tricky* topic. If you need any assistance, feel free to *Contact* (Appendix J, on page 178) the author.

Part III

More from Eclipse

## CHAPTER 10

Configuration Management

Eclipse is pug-in based. It supports a lot of popular configuration management systems through this plug-in based system.

10.1 CVS

CVS (http://www.nongnu.org/cvs/) is supported out of the box from Eclipse. See Eclipse wiki (http://wiki.eclipse.org/index.php/CVS_FAQ) and Eclipse help (http://help.eclipse.org/-help32/topic/org.eclipse.platform.doc.user/gettingStarted/qs-60_team.htm) directly for an indepth overview on CVS from Eclipse.

10.2 Subversion

There are two *different* plugins available to use Subversion from Eclipse.

- **Subclipse (http://subclipse.tigris.org/) is from the original** developers of Subversion.

- **Subversive (http://www.eclipse.org/subversive/) is hosted inside** Eclipse.org.

Which one to choose? It is a matter of personal taste. Any reasoning to justify one over the other would result into flame wars.

Both the plugins are developed, maintained and supported by the respective development teams. If you are an expert user of either of them, there is no need to switch. If you are just a beginner, either of them is fine.

Tip: Subclipse or Subversive

If you don't know which feature is missing in either of the plug-in, you are not missing any thing.

If you know which feature you are missing, you have already made the choice.

10.3 git

Git (http://git-scm.com/) is supported via a plugin called EGit. (http://eclipse.org/egit) See EGit Documentation (http://eclipse.org/egit/documentation/) for in-depth help.

10.4 Mercurial

Mercurial (http://mercurial.selenic.com/) is supported via MercurialEclipse (HG Eclipse) (http://www.javaforge.com/project/HGE)

10.5 Other SCMs

See the Eclipse Marketplace list of plugins on SCM (http://marketplace.eclipse.org/-taxonomy/term/26)

## CHAPTER 11

Code Review - Jupiter

Jupiter Eclipse Plugin (http://code.google.com/p/jupiter-eclipse-plugin/) is an excellent plug-in for code review right from within Eclipse.

For more details, download the latest UserGuide from Jupiter project download list. (http://code.google.com/p/jupiter-eclipse-plugin/downloads/list) (Current latest UserGuide was last updated on June 2009 (http://jupiter-eclipse-plugin.googlecode.com/files/UserGuide-06272009.pdf))

CHAPTER **12**

Task Management (Mylyn)

Mylyn is a new paradigm in software development — Task focused development.

It greatly reduces information overload and makes multitasking easy. It synchronizes with a variety of Defect Tracking tools like Jira (http://www.atlassian.com/software/jira/) / Mantis (http://www.mantisbt.org/) / Bugzilla (http://www.bugzilla.org/) and integrates development context with the incoming tasks from the defect tracking tools. (See Eclipse Wiki on Mylyn Extensions (http://wiki.eclipse.org/index.php/Mylyn/Extensions) for a list of external tools integrated with Mylyn.

You can find more at Mylyn Eclipse Page (http://www.eclipse.org/mylyn/)

Note: Explaining Mylyn in words is very tricky. Seeing a screencast/video would be a better alternative.

Please Search for video of Mylyn (http://www.google.com/search?q=mylyn&tbm=vid) in your favourite search engine and see them.

Part IV

Advanced Eclipse

## CHAPTER 13

Multiple workspaces

13.1 Why?

Why would any one like to have multiple workspaces?

Why? is the most boring question. How is what we should look forward to. But for the impatient, here are possible reasons why multiple workspaces are a good idea.

Project Name

Eclipse has a severe limitation. It cannot have two projects of the same name in one instance/workspace. If you are working on different versions or branches of the same project, Eclipse would not allow you to keep them in workspace. Under such situation, you would like to have different workspaces.

Shared installation

If the complete development team uses same installation of Eclipse, every developer should not be allowed modify the configuration stored in Eclipse. For these reasons explicitly mention your workarea in command line parameter.

Too Much Clutter

Possibly, you are a very big fan of Eclipse and you would create every project in eclipse. If your default Eclipse installation has many projects, you may choose to group projects and make them part of different workspaces.

Workspace settings

Few settings are stored by default in workspace. If you are working on different project with different requirements, you may choose to use different Workspace.

e.g. Eclipse settings on using *White Spaces* (Section 8.11, on page 130) is stored in workspace. If your projects use different settings, it would be advisable to use different workspace for these projects.

13.2 Set workspace via Command Line

The command line parameter for workspace is `--data`

If you run Eclipse as **eclipse -data d:\eclipse.workspace**, Eclipse would start using the workspace as `d:\eclipse.workspace`

13.3 Create a Desktop shortcut for Workspace

If you want to create Windows shortcut to start Eclipse with default shortcut,

1. *Right Click* on the Windows Desktop
2. Select *New → Shortcut*
3. Select *Browse*. Point to the Eclipse executable
4. Add `-data D:\eclipse.workspace2`

The newly created shortcut will use `D:\eclipse.workspace2` as the default workspace.

13.4 Create preferences to use a default workspace

You can either choose a default workspace, or let Eclipse ask you every time to choose a workspace (if you do not specify which workspace to be used).

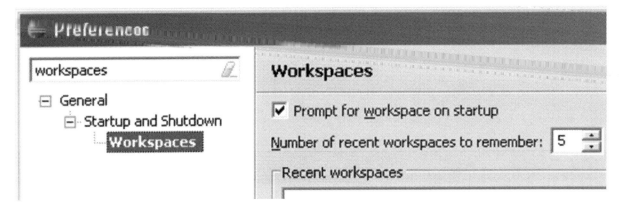

Figure 13.1: Eclipse preferences to select startup workspace behaviour

## CHAPTER 14

Upgrading Eclipse

Upgrading Eclipse is very easy....

1. First take a backup of your *Eclipse workspace* (Section 5.1, on page 30) *(Just in case.)*

2. Make sure you are connected to internet

3. If you are behind a network proxy, set it correctly in *General → Network Connections*

4. Press *Help → Check for Updates*

5. Eclipse would tell you about available updates

6. Select what you want to update, Click *Next* button

7. Accept License Agreement, Click *Next* button

8. *Easy!!!*

CHAPTER **15**

Plugins

15.1 Check if plugin is installed

How to check if a plugin is already installed or not? Which version?

1. Goto *Help → About Eclipse*

2. open *Installation Details*

   There are various tabs in the window.

   - Installed Software — An outlined overview

   - Installation History — A history of what was installed. When. An option to Revert is also available here.

   - Features — List of installed *Features* (Appendix A, on page 161)

   - Plugins — A huge list of installed plugins

   - Configuration — The running *configuration* (Appendix A, on page 161).

15.2 Installing new plugins

This is explained in detail in *chapter on extending Eclipse*. (Chapter 16, on the facing page)

Extending Eclipse

Change Eclipse to behave the way you like it to behave.

16.1 Installing a new Plugin

Note: If you are behind a network proxy, set it correctly in *General → Network Connections*

Eclipse Market Place

From within the Eclipse GUI, this is the best way to install/update a plugin.

Got to *Help → Eclipse Marketplace*

You will be taken to nice window to choose a variety of Eclipse Plugins

Eclipse Update Site

This is the old way of installing a new plugin via Eclipse GUI.

1. Press *Help → Install New Software*
2. Press *Add*
3. Give *Name* and *Location* of the Repository URL

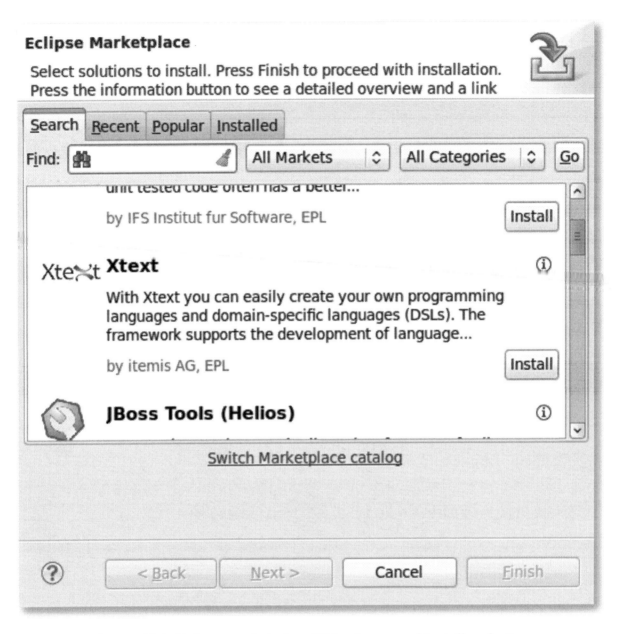

Figure 16.1: Eclipse market place UI to choose and install a plugin

Every Plugin has a *repository* URL. This is also called the *Update URL*

e.g. http://jupiter-eclipse-plugin.googlecode.com/svn/trunk/site/ is the update URL of Jupiter Eclipse Plugin (http://code.google.com/p/jupiter-eclipse-plugin/) [1]

4. Eclipse would download information from the Repository URL.

5. Select the relevant Plug-ins

6. Press *Next*

7. Accept the license agreement and press *Next*

8. Eclipse would ask to restart... Please agree

9. Now the plug-in would be available with your Eclipse installation

Steps similar to above are shown in *Installing CDT* (Section 16.2, on the current page)

Via Dropins (Dirty Way)

http://wiki.eclipse.org/Equinox_p2_Getting_Started demonstrates ways to install a new plug-in to Eclipse.

It is as easy as copy files to a specific folder and re-starting Eclipse:

```
eclipse/
        dropins/
                emf/
                        eclipse/
                                features/
                                plugins/
                gef/
                        eclipse/
                                features/
                                plugins/
                ... etc...
```

16.2 Installing CDT

If your Eclipse installation already has CDT, this chapter can be skipped. Else, follow the steps in this chapter to *extend* your installation of Eclipse to have *C/C++ Software Development* functionality.

---

[1] Jupiter is a code review plug-in tool for the Eclipse IDE.

(If you are not sure if CDT is already installed, please refer this section to check if plugin is installed. (Section 15.1, on page 146))

1. Go to *Help → Install New Software*

2. If you do not find something like `cdt` in `Work with` input Box, add CDT to `Available Software Sites`

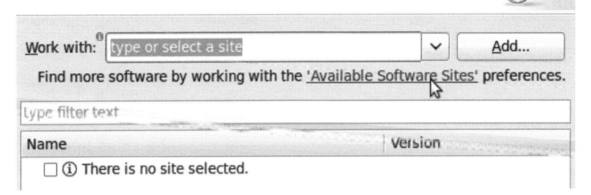

Available Software

Select a site or enter the location of a site.

Work with: ⓔ [type or select a site] ⌄ [Add...]

Find more software by working with the 'Available Software Sites' preferences.

[type filter text]

Name	Version
☐ ⓘ There is no site selected.	

3. Enable the CDT Repository in `Available Software Sites`

Available Software Sites

[cdt]

Name	Location		Enabled
CDT	http://download.eclipse.org/tools/cdt/releases/galileo		Enabled

4. Select the CDT Repository in `Work With` input box

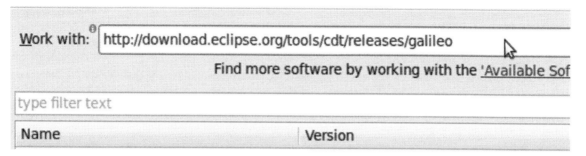

Available Software

Check the items that you wish to install.

Work with: http://download.eclipse.org/tools/cdt/releases/galileo

Find more software by working with the 'Available Sof

type filter text

Name	Version

5. Select the main CDT Plugin for installation.

Available Software

Check the items that you wish to install.

Work with: http://download.eclipse.org/tools/cdt/releases/ ∨   Add...

Find more software by working with the 'Available Software Sites' preferences.

type filter text

Name	Version
▽ ⊟ ▨ CDT Main Features	
☑ ⚙ Eclipse C/C++ Development Tools	6.0.2.201002161416
☐ ⚙ Eclipse C/C++ Development Tools SDK	6.0.2.201002161416
▷ ☐ ▨ CDT Optional Features	

6. Click *Next* button

7. *If you agree*, accept the license agreement and Click *Next* button

8. Eclipse would ask to restart... Please agree

9. Now CDT is available with your installation

16.3 Change the Splash Screen

The default Splash screen is not your type? Do you want to replace it? Change it to show your persona? Just create a BMP file and tell Eclipse to use it.

Open `eclipse.ini` change the *-showsplash* e.g.

```
-showsplash
C:\eclipse\meera.splash.bmp
```

Keyboard Shortcuts

Keyboard shortcuts make developers/programmers productive. The support for keyboard shortcuts is feature rich in Eclipse.

Press `Ctrl + Shift + L, Ctrl + Shift + L` (`Ctrl + Shift + L` twice). You will get the keyboard shortcut lists window

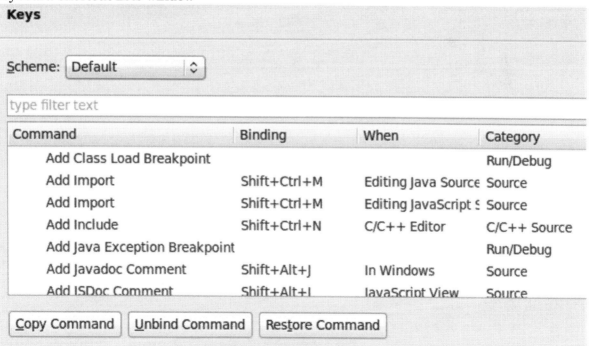

17.1 Schemes

The default scheme is the set of shortcuts of Eclipse. For users migrating from other IDEs (like EMACS/MSVC), Eclipse can be configured to use those shortcuts.

17.2 Context Sensitive

The keyboard shortcuts are context sensitive. e.g. while editing text `Alt + Down` moves line down. While in text views, it goes to next unread tasks.

17.3 Search Existing Keyboard Shortcuts

Its difficult to remember so many keyboard shortcuts. But in Eclipse, you can easily search for the shortcuts. Just press `Ctrl + Shift + T` twice, and type in the filter. Here is an image of searching only for `hierarchy`

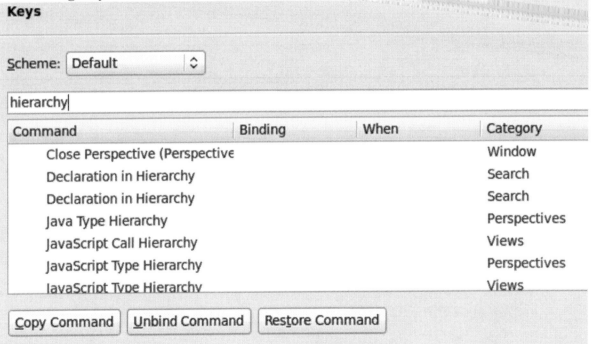

You can also see the description.

17.4 Create New Keyboard Shortcuts

For pre-existing actions, user can also create new keyboard shortcuts.

1. Select the command from list

2. Select *Binding* and key in the shortcut

3. If needed, select *When* that shortcut should be active.

4. If the keyboard shortcut has a conflict, it would be triggered in *Conflicts*. (So that you don't make mistake of assigning same keyboard shortcuts to more than one thing)

17.5 Update/Extend Existing Keyboard Shortcuts

Just like *Create New Keyboard Shortcuts* (Section 17.4, on the current page), you can update existing keyboard shortcut.

17.6 Multi Key Keyboard Shortcuts

Pressing Ctrl + Shift L once opens a preview of keyboard shortcuts. Pressing Ctrl + Shift L twice (Ctrl + Shift L, Ctrl + Shift L) opens the preferences on keyboard shortcuts. , is the delimiter.

17.7 Different Keyboard Shortcuts

What if you want to use "Different" keyboard shortcuts for the same operation?

1. Select the command

2. Press *Copy Command*

3. Now you have different keyboard shortcut. Just update this shortcut/command as described in *Create New Keyboard Shortcuts* (Section 17.4, on this page).

17.8 Delete/Revert Keyboard Shortcuts

What if you want to delete all the keyboard shortcuts/customizations, press *Restore Defaults*

## CHAPTER 18

Common issues

Here is a list of some of the common issues faces while working with Eclipse.

18.1 How to monitor amount of memory Eclipse is using?

Go to *Window* → *Preferences* → *General*

Enable the check box — *Show heap status*

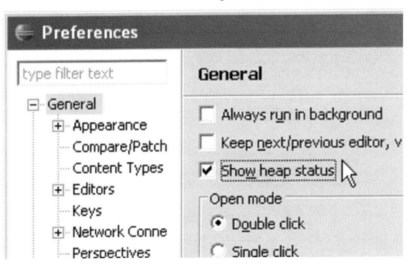

18.2 How to change the look and feel of Eclipse?

Go to *Window* → *Preferences* → *General* → *Appearance*

There are many permutations/combinations to try out.

This is the setting used for this book.

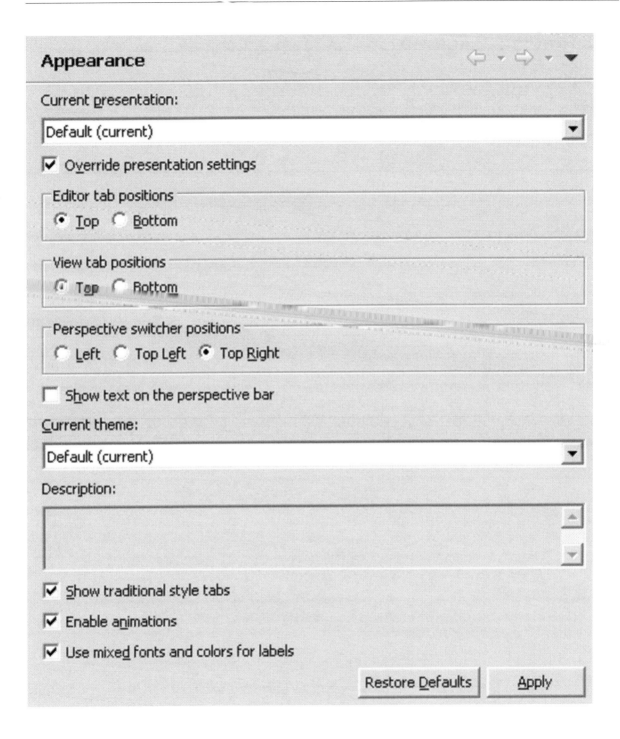

18.3 Eclipse is too slow!

- Upgrade Java
- Give more memory to Java/Eclipse (See *Modifying default start-up settings* (Section 3.7, on page 22))

18.4 More questions?

More common questions / FAQs can be seen at http://wiki.eclipse.org/-The_Official_Eclipse_FAQs

Or *Contact* (Appendix J, on page 178) the author if you have any other question.

Part V

Appendix

Acronyms/Glossary

(sorted alphabetically)

CDT C/C++ Development Toolkit. More at http://eclipse.org/cdt

Cygwin (todo:: add more on Cygwin here.)

Eclipse Configuration The current running configuration of Eclipse. Which plugins are loaded. From which location. Which version? What are the *JVM* (Appendix A, on the current page) Parameters, etc.

Eclipse Features A logical superset of plugins. e.g. Eclipse CVS Client is a `Feature`. There maybe separate plugins to provide ssh, ssh2, user interface, core functionality.

Eclipsepedia The Wiki (http://wiki.eclipse.org/) maintained at http://eclipse.org

EPL The Eclipse Public License. The license can be accessed at http://www.eclipse.org/-org/documents/epl-v10.php

GNU http://www.fsf.org/ , http://www.gnu.org

GPL *GNU* (Appendix A, on this page) General Public License

IDE Integrated Development Environment

Indexing Parsing C/C++ source code in advance to provide faster navigation, searching within code tree.

Java Virtual Machine *JVM* (Appendix A, on the current page)

JVM (todo:: Add what a JVM is here) More at http://www.java.com

LGPL *GNU* (Appendix A, on this page) Lesser General Public License

Mercurial Mercurial Distributed SCM (http://mercurial.selenic.com/) (The SCM used during development of this book.)

MinGW Minimalist GNU for Windows. More at http://www.mingw.org, http://mingw.org/wiki/MinGW, http://mingw.org/wiki/FAQ

MSVC Microsoft Visual C

UnxUtils Ports of common GNU utilities to native Win32. More at http://unxutils.sourceforge.net/

More entries are at *Eclipsepedia* (Appendix Λ, on page 161) Glossary (http://wiki.eclipse.org/Glossary)

Different formats of the book

This book is available in multiple formats.

B.1 Online web edition

The online version of the book can be accessed at http://eclipsebook.in (Earlier, it was hosted at http://book.dehlia.in/c-cpp-eclipse/ .)

- The online version is *free* for public viewing and sharing.
- *Few sections* of this book are not available online.

B.2 Printed PDF

This format is generated specially for the print media. References to the figures/sections/page numbers are explicitly numbered.

> *JVM* (Appendix A on page 131)
>
> External URLs are presented using the following printed and web medium)
>
> Eclipse (http://eclipse.org)
>
> References to sections and chapters are presented
>
> *Introduction* (Part I on page 8)

Refer to eclipsebook.in/appendix/buy-printed-book/ (http://eclipsebook.in/appendix/buy-printed-book/) for methods to get the Printed Copy

B.3 eBook PDF

This format is optimized for Electronic PDF readers. It relies on the *Hyper-linking* facility of the reader for navigating around the book.

> *JVM*
>
> External URLs are presented using the following in printed and web medium)
>
> Eclipse
>
> References to sections and chapters are presente
>
> *Introduction*

Refer to eclipsebook.in/appendix/buy-ebook/ (http://eclipsebook.in/appendix/buy-ebook/) for methods to get eBook.

B.4 ePUB

Content re-formatted for e-readers is available in ePUB format.

Go to eclipsebook.in/appendix/request-preview/ (http://eclipsebook.in/appendix/request-preview/) to find out where to get the preview copy for your platform.

Buy eBook (PDF)

See eclipsebook.in/appendix/buy-ebook/ (http://eclipsebook.in/appendix/buy-ebook/)

Installing Tool-chains

Note: This is only needed for Windows.

You will need to install some necessary toolchains/utilities to make things easier.

D.1 Why?

Why don't we get everything out-of-the-box with Eclipse? Why one (or many) more step(s) to install other utilities? Why is Eclipse not shipped with every pre-requisite?

This *blame game* would not take us anywhere. Why is Eclipse not shipped with every pre-requisite? The same holds true for Windows? Why is it not shipped with a compiler by default?

But here is a quick (and dirty) rationale/overview:

1. Whatever you get from http://eclipse.org/ is under EPL.

2. Most toolchains are under GPL.

3. EPL conflicts with GPL.

This makes its difficult for toolchains under GPL or LGPL to be distributed from http://eclipse.org/.

So you will have to install *MinGW* (Appendix A, on page 162) or *Cygwin* (Appendix A, on page 161) manually.

To keep things simple, installation of MinGW is described here.

D.2 Installing MinGW

1. Download *MinGW* (Appendix A, on page 162) from http://www.mingw.org

2. *MinGW* (Appendix A, on page 162) would ask for options to be selected. Select todo:: gcc and todo:: make

   (*MinGW* (Appendix A, on page 162) is a set of tools. C/C++ compiler, gcj compiler, etc. get distributed with MinGW. We only need gcc and make)

3. It is recommended to select the installation location along with Eclipse. If eclipse.exe is installed as c:\eclipse\eclipse.exe, installing MinGW as C:\eclipse\MinGW would make things simple later.

   Else make sure gcc.exe is in path.

4. Rename mingw32-make.exe to make.exe

   Note: (The default Make utility in Eclipse is make. Renaming mingw32-make.exe to make.exe just once is easier than changing the property of every Eclipse C project)
   ---

5. Done.

D.3 Installing UnxUtils

Basic Unix commands like **rm**, **cp**, **mv**, etc are not available in Windows. Luckily, *UnxUtils* (Appendix A, on page 162) is at the rescue.

1. Download UnxUtils from http://sourceforge.net/projects/unxutils/

2. Add the location of wbin to path .

   e.g. If UnxUtils is unzipped to C:\UnxUtils, C:\UnxUtils\usr\local\wbin has to be added to path.

3. Remove the UnxUtils make utility.

Warning: UnxUtils also distributes Make. The version, 3.78.1, is far more out dated than 3.81 from MinGW.

D.4 Visual Studio Express Edition

Possibly, the compiler from *MSVC* (Appendix A, on page 162) is free for personal use. It is possible to use the compiler form MSVC. Eclipse can use the compiler form MSVC. More about using MSVC is *explained in the chapter on using MSVC* (Section 7.4, on page 107) But, Eclipse cannot use the debugger from MSVC.

Setting up Zlib Source

A small *Hello World* program is not enough to know all features of CDT. We need something substantially more. Something little complex. Some independent existing piece of software. For this the Zlib version 1.2.3 source code has been used in this book.

If you wish, you can also *learn by practice* and see *exactly* similar screen shots in your environment.

Setup the necessary toolchains (Appendix D, on page 166) (if required). The version of Zlib used in this project can be downloaded from http://sourceforge.net/projects/libpng/files/-zlib/1.2.3/

Note: As of 2010.04.19, latest version of Zlib is 1.2.5. Use 1.2.3 version for testing purpose only.

Try to build Zlib on Windows command line, with MinGW.

1. Descend to `C:\sw\src\zlib\1.2.3\zlib-1.2.3` directory.

2. Run

   ```
   make -f win32/Makefile.gcc all
   ```

3. For debug builds, run

   ```
   make -f win32/Makefile.gcc LOC="-DDEBUG -g" all
   ```

4. To clean the project, run

```
make -f win32/Makefile.gcc clean
```

If that is successful, follow steps in *Externally Managed Build* (Section 7.2, on page 101). If it fails, have a *word* (Appendix J, on page 178) with the author.

Credits

This work is indebted a lot of people. This work would not have been possible without the inspiration and vision of these peoples.

- Parents

  - For whom, genuine effort was more important then results.

- Sibling

  - Who showed me the true mirror.

- My Guru — Pinal Sir

  - Who introduced me to programming.

- RMS

  - From whose name, the landscape of Liberal Software starts.

- Donald E. Knuth

  - For the excellent TeX typesetting system

- Everybody behind Eclipse/CDT

  - For the excellent IDE

- Family & Friends

  - Who always gave me space in their hearts.

A lot of tools have been used behind this work. While each tool performs a specific part of it, all are equally important. I am not only the indebted to the developers of these tools, but also the community behind these tools. Many thanks to them.

Here is a list of tools used (in no particular order) [1]

- Eclipse (http://eclipse.org) — The book is about Eclipse itself.

- Sphinx (http://sphinx.pocoo.org/) — The documentation system used to create this book.

- Texlive (http://tug.org/texlive/) — The system used to convert the documentation into PDF and ready for print.

- Emacs (http://www.gnu.org/software/emacs/) — Not just an editor. [2]

- Mercurial (http://mercurial.selenic.com/) — The distributed configuration management system that has helped organize the work.

- *GNU* (Appendix A, on page 161) — A whole set of tools. sed, make ,etc.

- ZScreen (http://code.google.com/p/zscreen) — To capture the screenshots easily.

- Python Slimmer (http://pypi.python.org/pypi/slimmer) — To make html files as small as possible

- Some of the icons used in the web site are from http://www.famfamfam.com/lab/icons/-silk/

---

[1] **To err is human.** I am sure I have missed a lot of entries in the list.

[2] Both Emacs and Eclipse have been used for editing reStructuredText files. Emacs is better as reST Editor. Eclipse is better as in IDE.

Testimonials

A few *good words*, about the *good book*, from some *good users*

Note: In some cases, the feedback is not enlisted verbatim.

This book helped me to learn how to program C++ in Eclipse Platform.

It is very user friendly and has a good structure which accompanies the Beginners from the beginning to the end.

— Ervan Chint

Many many thanks to Meera. I was trying to run a project on Eclipse but could not do. I searched for some help in the Eclipse forum but could not find any clear and simple solution. At last I notice Meera's post which gave me a way how to manage all these in the Eclipse. Really the contents of this book are very nice and very helpful.

Thanks.

— Chandan

This book is the only one I've found that clearly introduce and make effective the use of Eclipse, beyond the C/C++ development. Congratulations!

— Oparti

The book is very lucid explanations and i think it is a must for all! Have been searching for something like this.

I convey my appreciation to the author for the great job done!

Thanks

— Vamsi Parasa

So far, I like the flow of content from learning about Eclipse (for beginners) to development with C/C++ and on to advanced features of Eclipse. I really enjoyed the fact that though I have been developing with Eclipse for some time now, I was still able to learn a few things that I did not know about when I read the Introduction. I especially liked the instructions for set up and running Eclipse for the Linux OS.

— Brett Patterson

Very very good. I am novice in Eclipse, it was happening hours looking for information, until I read your book, thank you very much, help is of great, ... A greeting and again thank you very much for writing this book.

— Duque

Trademark Attribution

The content in this book and its related web-site(s) (Collectively referred to as **THIS BOOK**) may make reference to trademarks requiring attribution.

Unless and other wise explicitly stated, **THIS BOOK** is only affiliated to and endorsed by the author. It is neither affiliated to nor endorsed by any Organization, or other human beings (living or dead) referred to in **THIS BOOK**.

The views expressed in this book are of the author only.

All trademarks are trademarks of their respective owners. They have only been used by the authors under terms of *fair use*. Utmost care has been taken to use the mandatory ™ or ® symbols in the first use of these terms, and to provide proper attribution to the covered trademark, any mistakes are accidental only and not intentional. Please bring any discrepancies to the immediate notice of the authors. The mistakes would be fixed in future releases of **THIS BOOK**.

For the designations for which the author was aware of a trademark claim, the designations have been printed in caps or initial caps and are enlisted in alphabetical order of their respective owners here.

`aptana` and the related logos are a registered trademark of Aptana, Inc. in the United States, other countries, or both.

`Eclipse` and the related logos are a trademark of The Eclipse Foundation in the United States, other countries, or both.

`Freescale` and `CodeWarrior` are trademarks of Freescale Semiconductor Inc. in the United States, other countries, or both.

Lotus Notes and Sametime are registered trademarks of IBM in the United States, other countries, or both.

Microsoft, Windows, Visual Studio, Visual Studio Express Edition are trademarks of Microsoft Corporation in the United States, other countries, or both.

UNIX is a registered trademark of The Open Group in the United States, other countries, or both.

Java and all Java-based trademarks are trademarks of Oracle Corporation in the United States, other countries, or both.

Wind River is a registered trademark of Wind River Systems Inc. in the United States, other countries, or both.

Other company, product, and service names maybe trademarks or service marks of others.

Build Information

The content of this book is generated from the following version of the book.

Book Version v0.8.01-cae5c6a

Last GIT Tag v0.8

GIT Hash cae5c6a12641b9f02c4c4c84

Ratatouille v0.5.03-cbc8dd1

Docutils https://github.com/purnank/docutils-code-html5epub3/

sphinx-doc https://bitbucket.org/poo/sphinx-eclipsebook/

Contact

Email book @ eclipsebook.in

Blog http://blog.dehlia.in

http://blog.dehlia.in/category/c-cpp-eclipse/

Linkedin http://www.linkedin.com/in/dehlia

Twitter http://twitter.com/LeanReligion

Snail Mail Meera P. Ghumalia & Purnank H. Ghumalia,

005, Aishwarya Splendour Block 2,

24th Main, J P Nagar 7th Phase,

Nr. Brigade Palm Springs,

Bangalore - 560078

State: Karnataka

Country: India

Noteworthy changes

K.1 v0.8.x (under development)

- Distributed to POTHI.com and CreateSpace

K.2 v0.7

- Copyrights extended to 2014
- Create preview editions for google play and iBookStore
- Prited edition available on POTHI.com
- [web] Upgraded to google universal analytics for webpage
- [web] Upgraded Google Custom Search
- [index] New tagline: The easiest...
- [introduction/eclipse-overview] Wascana is obsolete
- [introduction/workspace] Clearer refernece to future section of multiple workspaces
- [advanced-eclipse/upgrading-eclipse] Tell user to take a backup before upgrading
- [appendix/formats-of-the-book] Online book is only partial
- Migrated build and distribution system to http://www.purnank.in/ratatouille/

Index

Advanced, 73
Multiple, 78
View, 71
Within C/C++, 73
Within file, 71
Search Results
View, 78
Single: Search
Pinned, 78
style
code, 110

T

Type Hierarchy
View, 83

U

UnxUtils, **162**

V

View
Bookmarks, 87
Call Hierarchy, 79
Include Browser, 81
Include Hierarchy, 81
Macro Expansion, 61
Outline, 54
Project Explorer, 42
Quick Outline, 56
Quick Preview, 60
Search, 71
Search Results, 78
Type Hierarchy, 83

47047406R00103

Made in the USA
San Bernardino, CA
20 March 2017